PRIDE TO PROMISE

Overcoming The Challenges in Life To Receive The Promises You Deserve

BRIAHNA WILLIS

Foreword by CONTRELL HENDERSON

Pride to Promise

Overcoming the Challenges in Life to Receive the Promises You Deserve

Briahna Willis

Receive a Free Digital Gift!

Get access to devotionals, discipleship lessons and more!

www.briahnawillis.com/pridetopromisedigitalgift

To my family and friends, I love you!!! Thank you so much for interceding in prayer for my eternal salvation when I was out in these streets, I am forever grateful.

Thank you to everyone who has been apart of my life in every season because everyone has helped me to become who I am today.

If I have hurt you in the past, I am sorry and I pray that you could find forgiveness in your heart for my actions or words that were reckless.

SPECIAL THANKS TO EVERYONE THAT HELPED MAKE THIS BOOK A SUCCESS!!!

Pride to Promise

Copyright © 2023 by Briahna Willis
All rights reserved.

briahnawillis.com

All rights reserved.

All rights reserved. No part of this book may be reproduced or transmitted in any form or by any means electronic or mechanical—including photocopying, recording, or by any information storage and retrieval system—without permission in writing from the publisher.

No book can replace the diagnostic expertise and medical advice of a trusted health care professional. Please be certain to consult with your provider before making any decisions that affect your health, including your mental health, particularly if you suffer from any condition or have any symptom that may require treatment.

Scripture quotations marked esv are taken from the ESV® Bible (The Holy Bible, English Standard Version). Copyright © 2001 by Crossway, a publishing ministry of Good News Publishers. Used by permission. All rights reserved.
Scripture quotations marked (KJV) are taken from the King James Version. Scripture quotations marked (NIV) are taken from the Holy Bible, New International Version®, NIV®. Copyright © 1973, 1978, 1984, 2011 by Biblica Inc. TM Used by permission of Zondervan. All rights reserved worldwide. (www.zondervan.com).
The "NIV" and "New International Version" are trademarks registered in the United States Patent and Trademark Office by Biblica Inc.™ Scripture quotations marked (NKJV) are taken from the New King James Version®. Copyright © 1982 by Thomas Nelson. Used by permission. All rights reserved.

Please note that Diamond Mine Media's publishing style capitalizes certain pronouns in Scripture that refer to the Father, Son, and Holy Spirit, and may differ from some publishers' styles. Take note that the name satan and related names are not capitalized. We choose not to acknowledge him, even to the point of violating grammatical rules.

Conard, Scott. *Weight Loss the Jabez Way: 7 Keys to Adding Years to Your Life.* Improv, Ltd., 2009.

Hansen, Brant. *Unoffendable: How Just One Change Can Make All of Life Better.* W Publishing Group, 2023.

This book is available at special quantity discounts for bulk purchase for premiums, fundraising, and corporate and educational needs by organizations, churches, and businesses. For details, contact contact@diamondmine.media .

Published in the United States by DM Publishing, a division of Diamond Mine Media LLC.

Diamond Mine Media LLC
Little Rock, AR, 72204
contact@diamondmine.media

DM Publishing, a division of Diamond Mine Media LLC, and colophon are registered trademarks of Diamond Mine Media LLC.

Photographer: Jessenia Ellis
Graphic Designer: Christopher Kylin Williams

FIRST EDITION

Hardback ISBN: 979-8-9898428-0-3
Ebook ISBN: 979-8-9898428-1-0

Library of Congress Control Number: 2024912362

Printed in the United States of America

Table of Contents

Part 1 | Pride

Pride and Ego: REVEALED..9
Introduction..10
Chapter 0 | The Foundational Foreword..................11
Chapter 1 | IdolaTREE...13
Chapter 2 | I Take Pride..21

Part 2 | Making

Real Feelz...29
Chapter 3 | Walking Into The Closet.........................30
Chapter 4 | The Spirit Within.....................................34
Chapter 5 | Help Me..42

Part 3 | Breaking

Lost...50
Chapter 6 | Peace in Pieces..51
Chapter 7 | Trauma and Forgiveness........................56
Chapter 8 | Strapped Down.......................................61

Part 4 | Refiner / Refining

Ask and You will receive…Your heart back...............71
Chapter 9 | Feel to Be Filled......................................72
Chapter 10 | The Process...80
Chapter 11 | Silent Progression.................................86
Chapter 12 | Building Below The Surface................91

Part 5 | Promise

Step into the Promise..99
Chapter 13 | Step into the Promise........................100
Chapter 14 | Internal Promise First.........................104
Chapter 15 | SHIFT..110
Chapter 16 | Come Out...113

Letter From the Author

Watsup this is Briahna Willis! I am so lit for you big dawg! This is your first step to sustained healing, deliverance, and freedom that is required in the process to walking out God's promise for your life. As I give you insight on the things that God has entrusted me to go through to get to this point, I pray that you will see yourself in every chapter because I am just a vessel in which God chose to deliver this through the experience of my life.

The first book that I read after an encounter I had with God made me so mad. I then started to ask God, "Why do I have to give this up? This is not fair! I want to keep doing me though!" Can I encourage you that this is the very place that you will find healing. I pray that you will ask these questions, but then press through the things that you may feel to then allow God to heal within you.

I PRAY THAT YOU ARE OFFENDED BY READING THIS BOOK IN SOME WAY. What I mean by "offended" is, I pray that this book will be the very thing that displeases, upsets, or disrupts "your opinion", "your belief", "your truth", "your way", "your life", and/or "your flesh" because that is the very place that GOD needs you to be for healing to occur. If you need a Bible verse for this, I will explain everything as you progress in reading this book.

God loves you so much and cannot wait for the conversations that you are about to have with Him. I Love you so much and am so lit for the journey that you are about to embark on.

I am not here to judge you, but I am here to show you love through the first section, which points out what pride is. I know that a real friend is one that will tell you that you have something on your face, so I am that person to do that for you on this journey! I want you to walk in great wealth and honor to a different level, not in "poverty and shame that comes to him who disdains correction" (Proverbs 14:18) that has once kept you bound. To receive a different life result, open your ears to hearing something uncomfortable. I love you so much, and I cannot wait for your healing to take place in the presence of God!

Love,
Briahna Willis

Part One

Pride

Definition: ///PRIDE///

"Pride says, I will seek FIRST the desires of MY heart and let everything else be added onto ME because of it." -Briahna Willis

Pride & Ego: REVEALED

My Pleasure which feels like heaven
Though hollow for my name
My kingdom will come
My Will is always to be done
On this earth not aligning with Heaven

I give myself breath and get my daily bread and
do not forgive those who are prophesying against my will
I will lead myself into the promise and deliver myself from evil
For I am the god in control of my pleasures forever and forever.
again
PRIDE

The center of this word being 'I' describes who the center really is "I"
It is "I" pursuing
PRIDE

Even the Greek word describing ego means "I" or "self"
Yet I seek to bring pleasure to arousing it daily
I control and tame mySelf
EGO

I devote myself to the idea of Self
Self-love, Self-Care, Self-Help
When I can't even help myself from falling
I fall on my face and become the "I" that
picks myself up again and again

I block my eyes from the Hill that has My Help
Now Blindly forgetting that The Creator of the Universe is my Help
I am clearly seeing physically…me
But Pride Full and stubborn to spiritually seeing Your Majesty,
the King who reign for all eternity

I block my eyes from The Truth because
I try holding my truth in the palm of my hands
It is my wisdom that reigns over all people

He said, "you will find true understanding and knowledge,
when you Fear the Lord", so really you are foolish!
Because you say you fear nothing
You call yourself the lord of your life so obviously there is no fear of The Lord
The one who makes darkness tremble
The one who set the stars into place
But you place yourself on the throne and became a child of…
PRIDE

So, Realize witcho Real Eyes the Real Lies you have been
fed by the tree you have eaten from daily.
Don't continue to be blind to the "I" that lies in the middle
Instead, just Open them to receive the Promise that is really simple.

It only comes through one King who gives you a robe and ring
This King makes you an heir
You will declare and overcome as you receive…
the Promise

BRIAHNA WILLIS

Introduction

Philippians 1:6

    This is not a book about overcoming "gayness" because there isn't such a thing; instead, I will discuss, through sharing my testimony, how to uproot not the stem nor the branch but the root, which applies to everyone and everything. I have heard a lot of stories about "I am not gay anymore because God saved and delivered me," and I leaned in to listen because it is a beautiful thing to know God and experience Him in such ways, and seeing this helped me. I have always been the type to see the big vision of things, so I asked God for a revelation when I completely gave my life to Him on January 9, 2022. I had a dope vision that God revealed to me after asking Him to show me the bigger picture of this new world. He opened my spiritual eyes to see a big tree that had already been established in the past and someone going up to tear it down by ripping leaves, breaking stems, and cutting off little branches. He then told me, "My people have been tearing down the leaves, stems, and branches, but there is a root to this tree of the knowledge of good and evil that has not been uprooted yet." I asked, "Ard (Alright), so what is the root then, big dawg?" He spoke one word that echoed in my soul: "PRIDE." Later, He told me the book title, and I have been writing gradually as the revelation came for years now to give you what you are able to read, which is an experience that God has blessed me with to "overcome by the words of this testimony."

Revelation 12:11

In this book, we are going to uproot the tree altogether, so get ready to overcome the challenges of life and progress toward the promises that you deserve!

Chapter 0:

The Foundational Foreword

CONTRELL HENDERSON

Our Heavenly Father is infinite in how He utilizes the concept of irony. The way He allows circumstances to come back full circle, hence the idea of the number zero. Interestingly enough, one might say, "Zero has no value". However, this is only true until you recognize the substance it contains. The concept behind this thought can be applied to an individual, a relational bond, or a question.

Speaking of questions, the often-overlooked value of these ideas happens to be a prime example of the Father's infinite irony. Who knew that a question would lead to an inspirationally empowering bond in Christ that would challenge theological norms? This is the epitome of the fellowship I've been honored to experience alongside of the author Ms. Briahna Willis. In a society that somewhat frowns upon the idea of questioning the things of God, my sister's humility, inquiry, and obedience has allowed the room for Him to intervene in her life for the sake of the Kingdom. How one might ask? It's largely in part to the audacity and redemptive power of questions and seeking to know the heart of the Father.

In Ecclesiastes 7:13, it reads "Consider the work of God: for who can make that straight which he hath made crooked?"

Again, if we examine the overlooked value in this question, it brings about more questions. These may include: Has pride caused the body of Christ to overlook the depths of the redemptive power of grace, salvation, and deliverance for all that humble themselves before the Most High God? Have we considered that self-righteousness may not only stand in our way of progression, but also in the way of the progressive spiritual path of others?

From Pride to Promise purposes to take us on a journey through the author's deliverance to explore these questions from a heartfelt perspective. We will ponder on how the body of Christ may have reduced the destructive nature of pride to simply a declarative name of a ceremonial and ritualistic month dedicated to homosexuality and gender identity, yet disregard its overall effect on the identity of the believer at large. It is a redemptive story of a young sister's revelation of our Heavenly Father's reconciliation process. May all who read be blessed and be inspired in the quest for God's presence.

Chapter 1:

IdolaTree

You First!

1 Peter 4:17

I was on the bed in my college dorm room with the smoke consuming the air along with another breath I was given, and at that moment, I realized a lot of things, the rest would be talked about soon, but the most prevalent was that I was a sinner fasho! I realized, with my eyes now opened by the Creator Himself, that I was not able to do this alone and that I needed to be healed from the trauma and wrong patterns of the past. I was here with my mind lying prostrate while my body was arrested by something bigger than myself—the simple fact that I have a journey ahead of me was at the forefront.

For so long, I went through life feeling suppressed, depressed, and oppressed by the very things that needed to be overcome by a simple look in the mirror. It is an action that is simple but overwhelmed with the complexity of our past things that we either have suppressed or disassociated ourselves from. So many are afraid to look in the mirror because that will leave them alone with themselves, their thoughts, their unresolved trauma, and sometimes a voice that comes in the midst of that depressed state of being to tempt and taunt them. We will discuss this further in the following sections, but right now, I need you to take that uncomfortable step by looking in the mirror.

This is for you first! [laughs.] I know that is a little bit contradictory to the title "Pride," but this is for you first. I need you to heal first because when you allow God to heal your open wounds from the world, you can help heal someone else. Galatians 6:1 talks about those who are "spiritual," helping people who are overtaken by sin. So many times, people who are in the wrong spirit are trying to guide people—not to the cross, but into their chaos that has not yet been dealt with!

For God to rid you of pride, there is an inner work that He needs to do through you to even see yourself as being someone who sins and falls short daily.

I need you to know that God "knew you before you were formed in your mother's womb" (Jeremiah 1:5), and the only way to get an understanding of yourself and the changes that need to be made for your elevation eternally is for you to ask Him first. You no longer want to heal and grow, so you deflect things to other people to further suppress the feelings that have now been bottled up for years.

> **"You hypocrite, first take the log out of your own eye, and then you will clearly take the speck out of your neighbor's eye" Matthew 7:3-5**

I want you to look in the mirror at yourself first. I challenge you to sit down and read the first two parts, PRIDE, and MAKING, BEFORE sharing this book with anyone else. Allow God to start the healing process in you first! Yes, I said you first! You First need to know God as your Healer, "Wonderful Counsellor, and Prince of Peace..." (Isaiah 9:6-7).

> **You must look at You First and allow God to "search you and know your heart" Psalms 23-24**

So please do not sit and think about someone else who will benefit from reading this book first because that is the very thing that has become a comfort to you: deflection and suppression. Step into something uncomfortable; it pays off, I promise. The very moment I stopped pointing my finger at other people first and started asking God to show me more of myself was when He began to humble me.

IdolaTREE

We ate from a tree that was rooted in pride, big dawgs! Yes... I said WE, whether you're White, Black, or Brown, and whatever gender you identify as or pronoun you have, EVERYBODY! Well, I know for a fact that I can admit that I have eaten from that tree... a lot of times. In this chapter, you will see why we tend to do this as our default and believe me; it is deeply rooted.

So many times, we want to point fingers and blame someone else to ignore the problems we have yet to deal with in ourselves. If you are either listening or reading this, I need you to point at You First and see yourself in this historical yet life-shifting event that occurred at the beginning of time.

Genesis 2 & 3 is the birth of a very familiar event that most have heard, seen, or maybe referred to at some point. Adam and Eve were in the Garden of Eden. Eve stumbled on the tree in the midst of the garden, and the serpent met her there. This was the tree of the knowledge of good and evil. I failed to realize that for all these years of just listening to or seeing this event from other sources, they only viewed one tree in the middle of the garden. Meaning that "our hearts have grown dull, ears are hard of hearing, and eyes have been closed" (Matthew 13:15) from seeing and hearing the promise that is supposed to bless everyone. I say this because there were two trees in the middle (Genesis 2:9); two choices: Pride OR His promise.

Let me show you that the root of everything going on in the world of sin today is centered around PRIDE. Eve wanted to do something that would make her more like God, which came at the cost of bringing idol to herself by raising her to an excellence that was not meant for her and then feeding this idea of potentially being like God to someone else out of deception. Deeper so, Proverbs 6:16 tells us about "these six things that God hates and seven that are an abomination to Him: a proud look," being the first of these. The Hebrew word for proud is "rûm," which means to rise and exalt. This is what Eve attempted to do in the garden: rise to a throne she was not meant to sit on. The Hebrew word for pride is "gā'ôn," which means excellence and majesty. The only one who sits on the throne and is called Excellent and Majesty is God, not man. We ate from a tree that was rooted in pride, big dawgs, by being tempted and deceived into something that seemed good but instead brought consequences and curses.

After eating from the fruit, Genesis 3:7 says, "Then the eyes of both of them were open, and they knew they were naked."

What was opened to them was the sight of the world, but a closing of their spiritual eyes transpired. They could no longer walk with God in the promise of having sight of it, but now they had to trust Him in the unseen by having faith because they were no longer able to see. They were blinded, which is why Hebrews 11:1 says,

"Faith is the substance of things hoped for and the evidence of things not seen." Hebrews 11:1

We know that they no longer saw and fell into pride because Proverbs 16:17–18 says,

"Pride goes before destruction and a haughty spirit before a fall." Proverbs 16:17-18

The story of Adam and Eve is described under the title in the KJV as "The Fall" for a reason.

The fall of man was rooted in PRIDE because it describes it as a fall. Since they fell, that means PRIDE blinded them from seeing the things that came after, like blaming God and pointing fingers at everyone else but yourself. Doesn't that sound familiar? Because of pride, we always blame God for things instead, which leads to destruction, and us asking God, "Why would you do this to me?" "Why would you make me this way?" This now leads to having a haughty spirit, which in Hebrew means exaltation, and because spirits are people and personalities without a physical body, it would be an exalted spirit that leads to the fall.

Every sin is caused by the curiosity of exaltation or pride in oneself by receiving some object, person, thing, ritual, place, or idea that will look appealing to "benefit" that person but is corruption to your spirit.

Simply put, Eve fell for the illusion to exalt the pleasure of what that object could potentially bring her and Adam instead of trusting that God knew and had her best interests at heart.

The moment Eve and Adam took a bite of that fruit was the very moment we saw them become blinded by pride. How? In Genesis 3:12, Adam was bold enough to blame God for something that he did. If that isn't deflection, I don't know what is. That is the very thing I once did often because I was blinded to seeing my faults. I blamed God for everything. I saw people as sin-filled and myself as pure. This is the very thing we fell into doing: IDOL A TREE! We made pride our idol from the beginning. We see other people as the problem without even looking at ourselves first. We look at the way other people decide to walk into sin, and the moment it looks different than ours, in which you are blinded to seeing, you now fall into the other 6 things that God hates (Proverbs 6:16–19), by judging them to further mask the things that you have yet to allow God to deal with in you first.

Proverbs 16:17-18 says, "The highway of the upright is to depart from evil: he that keeps his way preserves his soul. Pride goes before destruction, and a haughty spirit before a fall."

Let me break this thing down for you, as God showed me. If you want a life that is honorable and truly free, you must leave the things binding your soul and diminishing your spirit to protect your eternal soul and salvation.

Eating from a tree rooted in pride blinds your spiritual eyes, and that will lead to destruction due to a lack of seeing.

When you walk around blind, you will not see the destruction that is occurring or has occurred. The destruction that was rooted in pride being the catalyst leads to receiving a prideful or "haughty" spirit that further leads you to fall into the other sins that God hates (Proverbs 6:16–19). The first one of those seven is a "proud look," so again, I say every other sin is rooted in pride. There is an order that is established even in things that God hates because having pride-filled eyes will get you to become "a false witness that breathes out lies and one who sows discord among brothers" (Proverbs 6:19).

We take pride in the job that we do when, indeed, God cursed us with it because we wanted to IDOL A TREE and eat from its fruit. We parade around the city with different denominations, organizations, and sets we represent, just to point a finger or a gun at someone else. We ate from a tree that was rooted in pride, big dawgs! Now, let's deal with the pride in ourselves to walk out the promise.

IDOLAME!

Exodus 20:3
Matthew 6:24

When you posture yourself in making anything your idol, from the tree rooted in pride, it opposes God's will for your life. You are now on the opposite side of God because He says, "You cannot serve another God but Him" and that "you cannot serve two masters."

When you make yourself an idol before God, you become numb to the things that you were supposed to feel in order for God to fill you.

You instead blocked God from doing the work by replacing Him with yourself. You were cut by people taking advantage of you, stabbed in the back by friends, or maybe broken by the things your family said about you when you were younger, and that caused you to push the people away from you who actually loved you because your view of real love was contaminated by those closest to you from birth.

From there, you decided to hold hands with darkness, to make sure that would never happen to you again, to numb yourself from feeling, or maybe you turned to drugs, alcohol, cutting yourself, suicide, sex, people, relationships, getting pregnant, anger turned to rage, murder, pornography, stealing, rape, manipulation, fraud, or selling things illegally. This is what I did. I ate a lot of these counterfeit "fruits" because it felt good in the moment, even though it was not good for my eternal soul. In the process of filling myself with these things and trying to take my life because it still left me empty, I realized with the real eyes that God has now opened that I placed myself over Him.

So, before we move forward, if you feel a burning in your chest, if you are crying, if you feel lost, if you know one of these is something you have done or are doing, and you need clarity as to why you have this moment, Holy Spirit/God, my best friend is meeting you RIGHT NOW. He wants you to know Him like I know Him. God wants you RIGHT NOW to allow

Him into your heart.

If you already know Him, put that PRIDE aside and pray this prayer as well:

Prayer

God, I Surrender. *I am sorry for continuing to eat from the tree that was rooted in pride. Open my eyes, Jesus! I am sorry for continuing to choose a relationship with darkness. I have sinned, and I am sorry that I have put myself, my wants, my desires, my opinion, and my truth before the Truth, the Way, and the Life, which is You, Jesus. I believe that He lived and died for all of my sins. I repent, I turn from these things, and I give up my way and give my life completely to You, God. Thank You for the grace and mercies that are new every morning! Thank You for saving me! Holy Spirit, I welcome You in. Clean my hands, purify my heart, restore my soul, renew the right spirit in me, and transform my life! I welcome You fully to be the Lord of my life!*
In Jesus' name, AMEN!

If you gave your life completely to God for the first time or even recommitted it to God, I am so lit for you! Congratulations and welcome to the family, big dawg! This is the best decision you will ever make. Best of all, your eternal soul is saved, and now you are starting a journey in relationship with God. It says in 2 Corinthians 5:17, "Therefore, if anyone is in Christ, the new creation has come: The old has gone, the new is here!" This means that because you have decided to give your life completely to God, you are now a new person, and everything you once were is gone.

I'll explain it this way: You were just in a very toxic relationship with someone (satan); you were chased down to every place you went on this earth to be either stolen from, murdered, or destroyed unless you gave him what he wanted—your soul. You had the option to stay in that toxic relationship or to choose a relationship with the one who knew you from the beginning. Which relationship are you choosing because the choice is yours—life or death? Toxic or healthy?

To be honest, the old Bri Bri would have chosen toxic because I was blinded by the toxic relationship that I was in with what the world offered me. If that is where you are now, I will tell you that it looks good now, but when I had to keep going back to having sex with another person, back to smoking weed, back into another relationship, back into lies/manipulation, back into pornography, back into selling drugs and alcohol, back into another side hustle, back into popping pills, back into eating more food, back into rage, and back into sipping lean, they were things that will still leave me dead and leave me numb inside with my soul crying out for something more. These things of the world are temporary, but salvation found in Christ Jesus is eternal. If you feel someone internally or externally telling you to go back and read that prayer aloud, now is the time to do so.

You Stopped Here to Pray

Since God gave you a clean slate, are you going to treat your new life the same? No, you pursue Him more and more for things to be revealed, healed, and transformed. You just must be open to the process that leads to the promise.

Chapter 2:
I Take Pride

Proverbs 11:2
Matthew 23:27

In the foundation chapter and the first chapter, we discussed what pride is and how we must look at ourselves first because there is a lot in us that is rooted in pride. If you gave your life completely to God for the first time or even recommitted it, again, I am so lit for you. Welcome to the family, big dawg!

From Default

Matthew 23:12

We were all born to take pride by default. Think about it: when we were children, we were trained and programmed to listen to the voice of people first and to trust their words. Well, I will speak for myself as a youngin. From the moment we entered this pride-filled and sin-filled world, we were told to obey the voice of man, which can sometimes be opposed to the voice of God. Listening and obeying people above the voice of God became a default that was set from the beginning. We were born into a pride-filled environment, and anything not transformed by the renewing of our mind by God will be transferred. By default, we were set to take pride.

Our default setting is to listen to people speak to us and to see them as the source, and when we speak, our default setting is with a destination of our words to be everything that person may need. When pride has not been removed as the root, sometimes we speak partial truth because our default has not been changed, and this is what satan did in the garden, he told a partial truth to Eve in Genesis 3. A lot of times our words may be sincere, but the words that were spoken can be invalid in the minds of many because of us not allowing God to change the posture in which we speak from, a pure heart. He needs you to humble yourself in order to be exalted because your words are powerful, but they are rooted in pride and the only way to change the default of your heart is to seek Him.

I will give you an example: you continue to feed "your truth" and "your way" the more you go to the counselor or therapist in place of "seeking first the Kingdom of God" and knowing Him first as your Healer and your Mind Regulator. I am not saying that you don't need to go to counseling, but what I am saying is that you need to sit with the Only One who knows you better than you know yourself first. Sometimes we can find ourselves unknowingly going closer to the comfort of man because of the default that was set from the beginning.

We go to people first to find answers and/or validation, and we go to our counselors and/or pastors first, only taking their messages spoken as the truth. We build these people into an idol in our lives and put them on this "unreachable" status, while in the process tearing down ourselves and become blind to see the ability that God placed also on the inside of you.

We have become comfortable being fed this knowledge while further being blinded by pride to a point of not even finding evidence of these words that were spoken for ourselves.

Pride is the root of this default setting and we continue to feed it as we draw closer to the world instead of drawing closer to God. This is an idol and default that cannot stand in the way of God's will for your life because the only way to receive true freedom is to go to God first and have reverence for Him. Change your default to Him because the moment you allow Him in, "anything is possible with those who believe and walk according to His plan for your life" (Romans 8:28).

According to Ephesians 2:1–3, we once "were dead in our trespasses and sin... and were by nature children of wrath." This means we all have the same default setting in this sin-filled world that we live in. This is what David said in Psalms 51:5, "I was brought forth into, and in sin my mother conceived me."

It is so important to know that you and I were born into sin. No matter who your parents are, you were still born into sin because we live in a sin-filled world. For a default setting to change in your phone, you must first know what the default currently is before you can change it. My default was sin, and that grew as I allowed my environment to further have an influence and ultimately change who I had become. This change that I allowed by my environment then turned into a history or record of religion, drinking, smoking, having sex with a lot of girls, lying, manipulating people to get what I wanted, paper chasing, and finding my identity in my sexuality and other labels, UNTIL God encountered me and changed my default settings of every application of my life, erased the history, and gave me everything new.

Prayer

God, Show me all my current default settings in each application of my life! I need you to change my default in every application of my life so that it glorifies you. I am seeking your Kingdom and your righteousness first, like it says in Matthew 6:33. So God, you can grow the fruits of the Spirit in me, which are "love, joy, peace, patience, kindness, goodness, faithfulness, gentleness, and self-control" (Galatians 5:22-26).

Thank you for it being done!

In Jesus' name, AMEN.

Change has to come first before we get to these next portions of the process of understanding pride because you'd want to read with your eyes open, to further be ready to receive healing, rather than reacting from your flesh and ready to hurt, tear down, and stay offended because you don't want to see You First! If you feel a sense of "who does she think she is?!", start back with the love letter I wrote just for you. The reason is that 1 John 4:18 says "Perfect love casts out all fear." For you to receive the love with which I wrote this whole book, you have to empty yourself of the fears that you have picked up from the world, such as agitation, stress, offense, anger, hate, anxiety, etc.

After this paragraph ends, if you feel some type of way, I need you to go back to the beginning and allow God to do the work in you before you move forward, and if you move forward before it is time, then that's on you, big dawg. Just because someone else finished doesn't mean that is your pace, which is okay. Everyone has a different process and timing in which things will be revealed, so I encourage you to be patient and "wait on the Lord because He will renew your strength" (Isaiah 40:31) and your mind as you go through the process to get to the promise.

... In It

1 Peter 4:10-11
Job 12:10
1 Corinthians 6: 18-19

To a deeper degree, and expounding on the last chapters, this next chapter is about a topic that is a covert seed but is continuing to spring up a harvest of pride to remain king of your heart.

Matthew 6:21 says, "Where your treasure is, there your heart will be also."

This signifies that I am still bound to the root in some way that is holding my heart back from experiencing the King of Glory. So, let's go deeper and address this because we are seeking full healing from God.

Every bit of residue that has been stored up of pride inside of you has to go now in Jesus' name!

I mentioned this thing in the first chapter, but let's dive deeper into all facets of these sayings: "I take pride in what I do, I take pride in my work, I take pride in it, I take pride in my country, I take pride in my ethnicity, I take pride in my church, I take pride in my family, I take pride in my truth, I take pride in my sexuality, I take pride in my city, I take pride in my organization, or I take pride in my denomination." Whatever you can fill in the blank of this Chapter 2 section is also where a piece of your heart is (Matthew 6:21), meaning it is not fully surrendered to the will of God. What you think is "small" is the very large internal and/or external vow you made that is possessed by the world and is holding you back from experiencing His presence and relationship with Him in a deeper way. Don't believe me? Bet! I will give you some examples.

READ MY LETTER TO YOU & PRAY THIS BEFORE MOVING FORWARD

PRAYER:
"God, remove any lens of the world or lens of religion that may be blocking me from seeing Your Word clearly. I ask that you open my eyes to see through the lens of Truth found in You. I give you permission to show me myself by using the Word of you, God, a two-edged sword as it says in Hebrews 4:12 (KJV) to ultimately bring healing to me."
AMEN.

BEFORE YOU READ MY WORDS, READ THE WORD OF GOD FIRST BEFORE READING

Church/Religion/Denominations

1 Peter 4:17
Matthew 5
Matthew 6:33
Matthew 12:13-14

We take pride in our churches to the point of division occurring. You take pride in it, so now anything opposing what you are being taught is wrong. Don't believe me? Why are there now over 45,000 different denominations (non-denominations included)? It is because people could not read the Living Word of God through the lens of letting it be healing and cutting. You have taken pride in becoming a member of a church and doing the 'work' to be in that covenant that is holding you back from becoming a Citizen of Heaven. So now, with blind eyes reading the Word of God, we encourage our flesh by finding division that agrees with what we want. Now, you take pride in "reppin," or representing your set—I mean, the GSMBC or Christiandom (which isn't a word)—to the point that you might as well go walk in the pride parade with the LGBTQIA+ family because you are more alike than you realize. Your letters that you take pride in, which can't be spelled out into something simple, now has you walking in confusion because of the pride that has blinded you. You are now sitting in a church building, no longer there to hear a word spoken to remove scales from your eyes, but instead having a pride parade every Sunday in your Sunday's best with nothing but pride to show the world who instead needs saving.

Read Matthew 5–6 [33, specifically in chapter 6].

Organizations: FreeMasons/Fraternity/Sorority
Matthew 6:24
Deuteronomy 11:16
Exodus 20:1-4

If you are in a fraternity or sorority or are a freemason, you have made a covenant with them, so now that is a god/idol. No matter how active you may or may not be, you have vowed that organization the attributes that God freely gave you, such as love, peace, and happiness. There is a block to an extent with God because you have already given parts of yourself, such as "love, peace, and happiness," to that organization. You are cheating on a big God with a small god and have chosen to take pride in it by representing the letters you wear, the signs you throw up, and the unique sounds you make over speaking about the goodness of God. You can't have both. I would encourage you to look at your booklet of oaths and vows that you made to see where that organizations name is in replacement of God's name or His character described.

Work/Gifts
Romans 1:25-26
1 Corinthians 1:31
Proverbs 27:1-2

If you have a job and/or a gift, examine this example to ensure you are not taking pride in it. Like the verses mentioned at the top of this section, God has given us gifts to "minister to one another" with. What happens is that you take hold of that gift and no longer use it to bring glory to God, but instead, you stand in the way, bringing glory to yourself. You then fall into pride by not even acknowledging the giver of that gift, which he left you to be a good steward of. The moment you take ownership of something that is not even yours in the first place, He can no longer bless you to the extent that you beg him to because you have made yourself the "lord" of the gifts He gave you to steward while you are here on earth. Now, you are doing all of this 'work' to accomplish something, but in the process, you are limiting God's ability to do the full work because you are settling for the half work you did. Your job is not something that you should praise more than you give praise to God. So many times, we make the job our "lord" unknowingly by growing comfort in the thought that they are your provider instead of God being that in your life. If you find yourself waiting for that next paycheck, which I did in the past, you have grown comfortable with that establishment being your provider.

Knowledge
Romans 1:25-26
Proverbs 1:7
Proverbs 3:7
Proverbs 26:12
Proverbs 27:2

If you take pride in someone whose wisdom surpasses your own, you can make that person an idol. If you find yourself searching for all this knowledge on all these things and boast in yourself without acknowledging God through your humbled heart, you have made the resources that God has blessed you with into your "lord." Your default needs to shift to seeking God for wisdom and understanding, and He will give you fruit from the Tree of Life instead of daily consumption from the Tree of Knowledge of Good and Evil. Do not allow the resources to become your source any longer because they are holding you back from receiving the fullness of wisdom that God has to offer. When you allow Him to be the Lord of your knowing, you are humbled that you really know nothing and that everything given is all God, and it will be seen through your heart being humble instead of haughty.

... Continuing

If you caught offense to any of these, you have just experienced God pointing out a covenant that was rooted in pride. Before moving forward, I will place a prayer you need to pray below for you to renounce and denounce the covenant and then receive and walk in a relationship with God, stepping out of the paths that lead to religion.

The thing about taking pride in something is that pride was never intended for us to take ownership of because we own nothing. So, we are picking up things that were never meant for us to carry instead of accepting and surrendering to the fact that "our lives are not our own and we are not able to plan our own course" (Jeremiah 10:23 NLT). No longer will we take pride in anything because the gifts that God gave us, as in Romans 12:6, are to bring glory to His name and not to idolize our own by taking ownership of something that was supposed to be used for Him. I will no longer pick up pride in the things of the world, but instead, I will take pride to the feet of Jesus.

PRAYER

God, I am sorry for taking pride in my _____,
I renounce and denounce any covenants I have made with any organization, any free Masonic spirit, any soul ties with a person, any soul ties to the spirit of legalism, the

*occult, and any soul tie I made to be a child of pride.
I break it now. In the mighty name of Jesus!
I take pride to the feet of Jesus!
I admit that I know nothing, and you know everything.
I now welcome You in Holy Spirit. God, fill me with your holy fire.
I want a deeper relationship with You. In Jesus' name, AMEN.*

Part Two

Making

Real Feelz

I felt Nothing...

Not knowing nor caring that I was in pain.
So focused on finding ways to be numb to it.
I became so numb that I wasn't able to
feel where I truly stood.
Layers of protection like socks that did not
allow me to feel my soles.
My soul and heart was so covered.

I easily grew into someone that was just trying to survive. REAL FEELZ
Numbing my pain, sorrow, grief, fear, and confusion of purpose
with just another dose of things that were available
to fill me temporarily EVERYDAY.

Filling myself with pills the world offered, sex, drugs,
girls, alcohol, pornography, money, and other things.
It was like taking shots with no food digested beforehand.
Throwing all these things up after time because
of this void not being filled within.

I felt everything Alone. REAL FEELZ
From every death, every heart break, every
rude words said, every lie spread.
Hoping I would overdose on these pills of the world that I digested daily.
Shoot I Almost Did!

I found myself looking down the barrel of a gun.
Chocked up on my words by the sharpness of the knife
ressed against my throat. Trying to kill myself until You
redirected my wheel.
And.... I still continued
Shot after shot, pill after pill, blunt after blunt,
girl after girl, and splurging in hopes
of finding REAL FEELZ.

Still, I felt empty.
A Void left unfilled.
So, I took another pill of the world.
Isolating feelings from the equation by only numbing myself.

Through Every void within my heart, I wanted to handle it.
Instead of doing what the Creator had created His Son to do for all of us! JESUS!
I got tired and then decided to give it ALL to You.

I had to let you in fully to detox my flesh of all of
the things that was once abrading my spirit.
The roots that once were withered...
Now produce roots of joy and peace that I can't understand.

The pills that were toxic and distracting to who You have called me to be.
Now flushed away because no void is here in this
sacred place that You now dwell.
With You, I lack nothing.

This is me being sensitive and vulnerable to my REAL FEELZ

BRIAHNA WILLIS

Chapter 3:
Walking into The Closet

The Wardrobe & the Lion!

    As children, how many times do we take a glance of curiosity at things in the house of generations before us that have just been covered without being dealt with? Did you walk into the things they left for you that they have yet to heal from for themselves? Substance abuse, incest, poverty, or maybe even seeds of sexual perversion that have been covered in the same house you live in.

What starts off as you innocently playing hide and seek turns into curiosity as a child that leads you to walk into that closet that your parents, grandparents, or great-grandparents just covered up.

You are now in the closet of curiosity as a kid, surrounded by the clothes and other things that you were told were sins, but because they are familiar from generations before you, they became comfortable to put on these clothes, your curiosity starts to give in to the ideas. This unknown closet was comfortable to you because you put on the clothes that were fit for this environment, so you continued putting on these new clothes in this closet as you go deeper in preparation of the unknown.

You then go further and further toward the things that you are now able to feel surrounding you because you allowed that door to become a portal that is now open to access for you to come and go when it feels comfortable to you. Not knowing that every time we walk back into reality, we bring residue with us. When someone makes you feel sad or mad outside of the closet, you now walk into that closet to put on a garment of darkness that was never meant for you to put on and further walk into this unknown land. It keeps you warm and becomes the very thing that you know as your protector, provider, and healer. As you go back out into the world, more residue of "coming out of the closet" of curiosity follows you until you become comfortable with leaving these clothes on for all to see. Now, you have a default that is set to be comforted by darkness rather than being comforted by the one that clothes you in royalty. We were all born into sin unintentionally. We find a closet full of things that have just been covered by our family for so long. What you decide to do after finding that closet is your choice after discovering it; either you walk into the closet and stay in the new place that is dangerous, or you can come out.

I chose to walk deeper into the closet, which has a brand-new world that is readily available for you to experience, until God called me to come out of the closet. This is where my life story begins.

I Was Born to Obey!

Proverbs 19:16

I was that innocent, unique, and bold child who grew up going to a baptist church in Little Rock, Arkansas, to parents who were not married but loved me in the way they best knew how to. I was an unexpected child, I had to be because there was a 17 year age gap between me and my blood brother and god brother. People said that I was a "combo baby," favoring the appearance of both my mommy and daddy, but I always denied it and said, "I don't look like my mommy, just my daddy." I saw them separately, but similarly, I noticed the freedom that they had that most people didn't and found out they were both entrepreneurs. Both worked very hard to serve people, and they enjoyed it very much. It was really inspiring for a little girl to see her parents happy doing what they loved with independence. All except one year of my schooling up until high school was spent at three private Christian schools, but I still grew up in a different environment than my classmates. Not the slums, but casually having nights of gunshots sounding in the distance, some more closer than others depending on whose house I was over, and I had at least 4 houses combined to stay at. I knew that I was different from an early age, but the thing that would come next really traumatized me and equipped me with knowledge seeing to what extent the call of my life was.

I remember clearly that I was just leaving my grandmother's house with my dad when I was just starting my school years. I was in the back seat of my dad's sports car, laughing while my dad drove down the hill to the house, when suddenly, a voice told me urgently, "GET DOWN NOW!" With a fear of that voice that I now know as the Lord God, I obeyed. My dad looked back at me with confusion surrounding his face, but not even 3 seconds went by before several gunshots rang out in the direction of the car, but we were both free from injuries. From that moment on, I knew that my life was important, not just to me but for God to use me. I was quiet about this and did not speak about it at all until recently with my mom because of the fear that I could not stay with my dad anymore. Now I realize that I was born to obey the voice of my Heavenly Father. He spoke to me and saved our life, but it took me being obedient from an early age. It was so easy then to not be bothered by what people thought and to have pride in the way because it was just obedience and an admission of knowing that you know nothing until your Father shows you. I was born to obey His commands to receive the promises that were in store for me.

So, I continued with my young life by going to school, going to church, and singing in the choir, feeling on the inside that there must be something more I could do to serve and worship the Lord God who protected me. I believed that maybe if I joined the church I grew up in and became more involved, I could worship God in a deeper way, but that changed nothing. A giving heart that I gained from both of my parents is what grew my heart to serve people, but I didn't feel that there was a depth or history that I had with God, aside from that instance, so I asked and searched.

I was 8 years old by this time on Sunday morning at the 11:30 a.m. service, and everything in my life was activated. I sat in the pew beside my mommy and looked around at people running and shouting, worshipping God, and I then knew what I was going to ask God to do. I looked up in full faith and said, "God, I am looking around and see these people worshipping you, and I pray that you will take me through things to truly worship you like these people are. AMEN." This dangerous prayer was the start of this journey, and I am now able to reap the fruit of today and the test I overcame in my life that has now been joined together to give you my testimony.

This life story is not about walking out of one thing but instead about how all the pride I had taken in pleasing my desires and finding my identity in these different titles and labels really set me up for God to radically open my eyes to the promise that He has for me.

Chapter 4:
The Spirit Within

I Was Born This Way

I was most definitely born different from the people I was surrounded by daily, whether at school or in the neighborhoods at every house I stayed in. I felt hidden in so many ways from the world. So many times, I was either watched like a hawk by my daddy while playing basketball with the boys in the neighborhood or just not allowed to by one of my grandma's, but I never understood the why, but now I honor it.

While in elementary school, I remember being over at my stepdad's house and being awakened to loud but familiar voices in the other room.

My loving mother came into the room I was in, and with a softly spoken voice that I knew was hurt on the other side, she told me to go with her, and we slept in the car that night. Later, they ended up separating, and my mommy and I were homeless, trying to find a place to stay. We stayed with my grandma for months until she had enough to get us an apartment. I was so excited. She surprised me one day after school with my room decorated so cutely, and God protected us in there because they would have units burn down often. I remembered walking in to see her room and seeing nothing but a little couch and her Bible study things beside it, and I grew confused. She got me this bed and decorated my room, which was so perfect, and then I saw she only had a small couch to sleep on. I asked her where her stuff was, and she proceeded to tell me, "I'm okay with this baby girl," and that was the moment that I understood what true sacrifice was.

Every morning around 4:00 a.m., she would be praying and reading the Bible, and one time, I woke up to hearing her in tears and conversation, so I wondered why God would take her through all these things, but a voice said, "She will be alright," so I stopped worrying. She had a picture up on the refrigerator of a champagne gold Buick Lacrosse, and one day, I asked, "What is this for, Momma?" and she told me it was her dream car that she was going to have. I was a puzzled little girl, knowing that I just saw nothing like that outside that she was driving in, but I watched her work doing what she loved to pursue what God had for her. Finally, she got the car and the house. I really saw what consistency in relationship with God and the result of faith looked like. She is and was a very powerful woman of God, which has impacted a lot of teenage girls' lives. The impressive thing was, lol, she still never allowed me to miss church, even if I wasn't feeling well; I was their rain or shine. My brother started staying until he got his business off the ground, and I was so excited! He brought a PlayStation over, and we would play video games all the time, and it was so fun, even with the age gap.

Days after school with my dad were usually spent going on dates somewhere, serving others who did not have much, experiencing new places in Little Rock, or hanging out with him while he worked. He was my coach in softball, and that man did not take any L's or very little, but I thought that was dope. Seeing his success with coaching inspired me to want to coach basketball later in life, but somehow, God made me a golf professional instead. My daddy was and is about the calmest person I know on earth because he would take me to games that he umpired at, and they would say stuff to him, and he just smiled at me because I was ready to fight about that one. Seeing this and other things showed me that he is a very intelligent man of God who would always talk with my guy friends in our neighborhood to give them guidance.

At school, I was either playing sports with the boys or, when I was with the girls, they would bully me and talk about things that bored me, such as dolls, wearing pink, and braiding. I did not like to wear dresses, and I still don't. I would rather have played with the boys because I was athletic, and the girls were not doing things I enjoyed. My grandmother said someone gave me a doll when I was younger, and I told them, "Thank you for the doll, but I'd rather have a ball." I was born this way, and I was different.

When you do not conform to the culture that you are in, they try to make you conform by placing a label on you that keeps you limited to what I became confused about: my femininity.

The lens that people see things through is filled with the learned traditions and preferences that the world has told them to believe, and people no longer have simple things that are defined, like modesty for individuals, instead the world has a list of things they can and cannot wear.

Imagine you tell a child, "You're a tomboy and you like to wear pants, so you must like girls," being said to you around the age of 10. I have always looked at women since I was young, but I didn't know what to do with those feelings the older I got. The moment people place a label on someone is the very moment you limit them, but not understanding that, I searched for that label deeper because I finally got a name for what I was going through.

I went to church one Sunday and saw this girl who was older than me but dressed the same as me. From this point, I asked her questions to hopefully find out more about myself, and what she said was few, but the actions showed a lot. I would then begin to watch her, seeing her appearance at church, and every Sunday, it became more apparent to the older kids that she was "gay." She brought her girlfriend to the church, and they talked so badly about her. I continued to show love toward her because we were more alike than she realized, but the haughty eyes and bullying overtook her, and she left the church for years.

They began to bully me at church, calling me names and talking about my outward appearance, so I slowly changed it to not being seen the same as she was. I started to question my identity and sexuality, but I decided to show people the church girl image more. I read my Bible to be able to quote it, and I followed the things that my church said were acceptable there. I still found myself crying myself to sleep with these kids' words as my last conscious thought before snoring because no matter how hard I tried, I was still alone. It was better knowing that they did not know who I was based on my outward appearance because I could not get bullied based on something they could not see. The things in my mind were now clouded by everything I had hidden and suppressed. I placed a mask on so the religion of the outward could hide my internal soul that was crying out.

My cousin was the choir director at my church, and years had passed since that dangerous prayer on that Sunday morning. I was in the back of the sanctuary and asked him if I could help him with anything before service; he needed something from the equipment room, so I went. I opened the door to see an exposed body beyond what I had ever seen. It clicked; I walked in on people having sex at church. Wait what?! Church. Yes, I couldn't believe people would ever be so bold in the wrong way like that. This became a perverted seed that was added to the thoughts of my mind, so I began to explore from there. I allowed this sexual spirit (a personality without a body) to dwell in this place. What I once saw in women was now enhanced looks, and looks at men were also perverted, but "I always looked and never acted, so I didn't sin," or so I thought. What I didn't understand then was that those very lustful looks became visions of sin that formed into actions that may transpire in the future. That personality began to show itself to me through my inner thoughts. Without that knowledge at that time, I continued to look, feeding what I thought were the desires of my heart, but really, it was a spirit within, woman after woman and man after man, but women caught my eye more.

I Was Born This Gay

We are conceived into a sin-filled world. In the same way that people resemble their parents physically, they can also do so spiritually. What I mean is, there are certain things that were generationally passed down that you have to overcome so the cycle/curse can be broken with you. There is always a root that needs to be broken generationally, and what I do know is that these lustful desires that I had for women were passed down through lust or perversion because I have always found myself looking at women since I was a kid. With no words to put to it then, but with an underlining knowledge, I accepted that "I was born this gay.

I began to explore sexually for some type of pleasure, so I stumbled on a lot of stories on this app, but my young mind became curious about the wrong things at the age of 14. I stayed up to five nights straight reading these sexual fantasy stories on that app, where I was introduced to the idea of women in my dreams and imagination. It then led me to explore my body and let my hands go where they led me. My feeling of being so confused and alone was heightened because I felt that no one truly saw me, but everyone saw me as "the church girl" on the exterior. I was now alone with my thoughts and the spirit within speaking louder than my own, telling me to do things that I saw by reading these stories. I was willing to fully allow this personality of darkness that I held with comfort to consume my body to get what I was now desiring. I was so familiar with this voice now; it was a distant but familiar voice that told me to receive pleasure that had no name but actions attached to a dog because I had to stay quiet to people about these things I was experiencing. I began to have visions replay in my mind of a dog licking me inappropriately and even got to a point of having a urge to take action to fulfill what I saw in this vision. Even though I was being led to almost go through this sexual act with a dog by this voice, I felt something holding me back from doing it, so I didn't go through with it.

Now, I was consumed with all these thoughts, and I felt like I had no one to talk to. I was alone and at the very place where I thought hope would come on a Sunday morning, but instead, it was met with rituals, shouting, and people bullying me. I found myself comfortable holding hands with darkness because no one showed me the light that I gave freely to others. As the months progressed, that voice that told me to play with the dog in a sexual way began to decrease as I started reading God's Word more. I realized that I needed to stop, I worked so hard to stop, and eventually, I stopped. I swallowed my pride.

The thing about swallowing pride, something that was not meant for you to have in the first place, is that it will always have to be revealed again because of certain triggers such as smell, words, and taste. With pride swallowed, I decided to mask these feelings by thinking of myself as a person who could be a healer and a miracle worker. I worked in my own will to give up something instead of giving it to God, so I slowly started to take pride in what I did. I no longer saw God saving me because I had become my own savior. Yes, the Bible says to take every thought captive, and there is a certain point at which those thoughts you don't take captive become very accessible for a spirit to dwell within.

Psalms 51:5
Behold, I was shapen in iniquity; and in sin did my mother conceive me.

It was now around the age of 15 that the prayer from the age of 8 started taking effect fully. The pride that I swallowed from becoming my own healer and savior then transferred into my other friendships, skewing the advice I gave. I was still the "church girl" externally that was masking this internal feeling that I was battling for being born this gay, so people received religion. As a result of this battle within my mind, I now had my two friends, who were girls, standing in front of me talking about going on a double date, so I proceeded to ask, "With who?!" They then said they wouldn't tell me, but one had given into my words because I wanted to go. They both then showed me a picture of two girls on their screens, and at that moment, instead of choosing to respond from my internal feelings of relating, I responded in fear of my mask for so long being revealed.

So, I chose to respond from the thing that has numbed me for so long, religion, by saying, "Oh, y'all are going to hell." That was the first and last time I said that because the journey that God took me on really removed my heart of religion and stone, and He replaced it with an understanding heart of flesh with my life moving forward.

> **I denied my feelings to the point of them being so masked that the only thing I offered people was religion.**

I did not want to reveal myself for who I was because I now had a religious requirement to uphold, so more bullying would not come from school and church. I became so consumed by religion after giving those sexual things up, and this is the very thing that God had to break in me to show Himself as my Savior, Healer, and Deliverer, even from the pride that I carried within.

I Was Born to be Born Again

John 3:1-21

> **Rituals overtook me to a point where I did everything with the thoughts of people in mind and never looked at anything I did as being for my eternal soul.**

I remember going to the altar call to become a "member" of the church because it was the declaration that people were no longer talking about my outward appearance. I got baptized because they paraded those kids that did into children's church like superstars, and I just wanted to be seen and be cool, and those things changed nothing.

I kept searching, I snuck to other churches, and nothing came off. I started then to grow closer in friendships with those and more individuals, and shortly after, I started drinking and smoking weed around 14 years old. I was searching for something that I didn't find in the church that I grew up in until they gained a power couple that became the youth pastors and a loving example in my life. They saw the light in me even when I was very shy around people, and they further challenged me by choosing me to be a part of a youth leadership team. I started to understand the importance of having a relationship with God, so I started to talk to Him more.

I believe now more than ever that yes, I was born this way, but now I know that, "Therefore, if anyone is in Christ, he is a new creation; old things have passed away; behold, all things have become new" (2 Corinthians 5:17). If you are confused about that verse, it's okay; my bro, Nicodemus, a religious leader from the Bible, was too. He set up a meeting with Jesus at night and asked, "How can you be born again if you are already born on earth?" What he did not realize is that to be born again meant, as Jesus said in John 3:6-7, "Flesh gives birth to flesh, but the Spirit gives birth to spirit. You should not be surprised at my saying, 'You must be born again.'"

I know you have been reading the verses at the top of each section because you would have peeped John 3:6 relating to Psalms 51:5 and Ephesians 2:2. We were born into this ghetto world of sin to flesh, which are people, because people have flesh, and to be born again, you have to be born in the Spirit, meaning you need another birth, and that only comes through believing and accepting Jesus Christ into your heart fully. A Scripture that a lot of people love is John 3:16, but we need to start reading the whole context of things.

John 3:16-21:
"For God so loved the world that He gave His only begotten Son, that whoever believes in Him should not perish but have everlasting life. 17 For God did not send His Son into the world to condemn the world, but that the world through Him might be saved. He who believes in Him is not condemned; but he who does not believe is condemned already, because he has not believed in the name of the only begotten Son of God. 19 And this is the condemnation, that the light has come into the world, and men loved darkness rather than light, because their deeds were evil. 20 For everyone practicing evil hates the light and does not come to the light, lest his deeds should be exposed. 21 But he who does the truth comes to the light, that his deeds may be clearly seen, that they have been done in God."

This means that in its entirety, God loved the world that He created so much that He gave His only Son, Jesus, to die for whoever chose to believe that they would have eternal life in the Kingdom of Heaven after being here on earth.

When you are born again, like Jesus was explaining to Nicodemus, God will renew a righteous spirit in you and give you a clean heart.

The more that you surrender parts of yourself to Him, the more open you are to the process that prunes you in preparation for living in the promise.

If you once checked off boxes of what religion has to offer like me and Nicodemus once did, you will instead walk in a relationship with God by talking to Him about everything that you feel, giving Him time to speak and heal your open wounds, and knowing Him as your friend. As you surrender through your words and in your heart, everything to Him that you have tried to do by yourself in the past but have failed or had the same ending result, just know that you are born to be born again.

Chapter 5:

Help Me

Believe Me

Matthew 12:43-45

I continued to hang around that crowd, and that pride I once swallowed was now back up, but this time stronger. I began talking to boys because my best friend had me on double dates with her, but I still preferred talking to girls and did not because of the fear still in me. One boy who went to my school and liked me reached out to me, but I just thought of him as a good cover-up, so I entertained him, but he wanted sex, and I didn't want that. So, there was only one option: I cut him off, so I thought.

It was one day after school that I was leaving class later because I needed help from a teacher, and it worked perfectly because my dad was running late. I walked out of the class, and it was only me and that boy in the hallway upstairs. I looked into his eyes from a distance and saw an emptiness inside of him, and I felt the need to walk fast after seeing the eyes of this familiar spirit. He ran after me as I got down the first flight of stairs. He caught up to me and pushed me into a corner with his pants unzipped, asking for something that I was not willing to give. I tried to push him, but he was too big, so I kicked him and ran. This really caught me off guard because I have always been cool with dudes, so why would this happen to me? Thoughts of who would even believe me came into my mind, so I kept quiet.

I was about to tell my momma until I went to go play video games at someone's house, and my mom let me stay over there because I had my car to drive home in the morning. It got late in the night, and the boy's father told me that I could sleep in his son's room, which was confusing, but I did. Dreaming was over, but my eyes were still closed because I had never woken up before to this feeling as if someone was in bed with me. I was frozen, growing numb second by second to the action trying to be attempted under the sheet. I was fully awake now to the boy trying to touch me inappropriately by pulling my pants down slowly, and I just sat there in shock. I conjured up enough bravery in the seconds after being fully alert to push him off me, and in the act of words about to come out of my mouth, the father walked in. He told him to leave the room, and I got up to leave that house and never returned.

As soon as I got outside their front door, I called my dad telling him what happened and I cried the whole drive back to my mom's house. He was furious because of the proximity this individual was allowed to me and was having to get talked off the ledge of doing something illegal. I got to my mom's house with tears in my eyes to see her on the phone with the father of the boy, saying it's okay, then telling the boy she forgave him. I didn't even tell her what happened yet, and she forgave him?! When I tried to explain to her, I was met with unbelief and certainty that what I said from that point on was false, so I shut my mouth and said nothing. I grew bitter in my heart toward all three of them because the first time that I spoke up, my mom didn't believe me and forgave them. I was so heartbroken, but I masked it with unforgiveness that dwelled there.

Behind that closed door, I was praying to God for the restoration of my mommy and me to have a great relationship because I saw my friends and families' bonds with their moms and just cried in desperation for the same. It became a routine: cry, pray, and see them together still repeat; OR cry, pray, and have another head budding with her and repeat. I grew more hopeless, but I kept the routine going.

I was zoned out of reality on another day without an answered prayer and wondering how I should have done something instead of freezing in that bed. I was made conscious when my guy friend touched me and tried to ask, "Bri, you..." but was cut off by my punch to his chest. He just shook it off and saw my eyes water and said sorry; he knew I never hit anyone before, and I saw an alarming look on his face. He calmly set his posture back and said, "What's going on Bri? What happened?" I cried in his arms and told him, and anger filled his calm spirit. He asked who, and I knew I could not tell him because he was really in those streets, as were most of my other friends, so I kept quiet.

I was in church, really expecting confirmation or something to help me, but I got nothing, so I called a guy friend and asked if we could have sex. I wanted to know if I should even mess with guys anymore after all these things had happened and because I was very curious about girls, but I didn't do anything because of what I was taught. I met with him and a few more boys, but knew I wanted girls instead, so I started searching.

Redirected Wheel!

Isaiah 38:16

A little time went by after I entered relationships with girls, and my first girlfriend cheated on me. I was hurting so bad that I got my keys and started driving. I was on the interstate, driving 80 mph, crying, and a switch flipped. I stopped crying, and something told me to go 120 mph like a speed demon, so I did because it intrigued the pain that I already felt. I wanted to kill myself at this time, and something was telling me, "Just do it already." I was about to accept the challenge, but I had a little ounce of fear in me, and with that, I said, "God, if You save me from this, I will follow You." And then, I let go of the steering wheel, seeing my front windshield direction turn toward trees, then suddenly, the bumpers redirected the wheel back straight. I proceeded to keep my word by taking a first step by immediately calling my pastor and his wife, and I went to their house to just talk with her, not about the suicide attempt but about the breakup. She listened and still loved me after telling her, and then we proceeded to talk and laugh until I left.

One of the nurses my daddy knew let me use the nurse's area to shower, so they forced me because I didn't want to leave him.

As he eventually started to motion for certain things, I knew that everything was going to be okay because I had faith. Waking up to that long rest, I felt joyful but also sad about this place that my dad was in right now. I felt like no one understood what I went through except Him, so I went to his house to get something, and that was when I started turning to other things, leaving the hospital often to go consume a drink or smoke because it numbed the pain of what was actually going on.

unlikely that he will live through the surgery, but we can try…" I heard a slow motion in my family saying, "Yes, try it." The doctor then said, "We can do it as soon as possible, but you may want to send two people in to see him, just in case. I will come back soon to see when you want me to start the surgery." I heard distant voices saying my name and asking my grandma to go see him, so I went in. I had never seen so many things connected to him before, and I began to speak to him, saying, "Daddy, I need you to pull through this because here, you are the only one who understands me and tries to. I want to go to the sushi place with you again, so please live through this, Daddy." I felt like a part of him heard me, but I was not certain. I got back to the room, and tears would not fall yet. The doctor came in with just 3 of us there and said, "We have to perform it right now because of the chances." Suddenly, his voice blanked out, and I heard the voice from earlier say, "In 5 minutes." I zoned back in to say calmly, "You can start in exactly 5 minutes on the surgery," so I signed some of the paperwork, and we prayed for the doctor while he was in the room.

After that, I went numb. Walking out the door, tears filled my eyes with every step I took as my aunt followed quickly behind me. I was crying uncontrollably in this long hallway, and the closer I got to a corner, the louder I became with my feet collapsed under me. My aunt was trying to console me to quiet down, but I could not control this cry roaring and whaling out of me. I sit curled up in the corner, mad at God. I sat there with my head between my legs and felt someone in front of me aside from my aunt, so I looked up to see this woman who had white on praying for me. I looked up, and the cry got smaller as she consoled me as if she knew what I needed. I look at her face as she talks, speaking calmly, "What's going on?" I proceeded to tell her, "My daddy," in a baby voice, trying to hold back tears and snot from being in her face. She sat for a second and said, "My father is here too, and He is doing a work," and I looked at her, confused and with a face saying, "Why did you say that? What does this have to do with your dad?" She understood my facial expression and told me three words: "Have Faith, Briahna!" and she walked off.

Those three words rang in my ear the entire surgery. We went into the big waiting room now, and I walked in to see at least 20 more familiar faces and more people including my friends were flooding in. It shocked me to see that many people were there for my daddy and to see that many people circled around to pray for him really shocked me to see his impact. Two hours had passed by, and it was on a weekday; wow. The doctor came in shortly after to tell us that he had made it out of surgery, but he was in a coma, and we must pray for him to wake up. He was in the ICU in a coma for a week or two. I stayed there by him, hoping that he would wake up and give me a sign. I believe I stayed in there for a week without showering.

it off and leave as that voice told me, and the teacher asked when I would present, and I heard that same voice say, "You won't be presenting; leave now, Briahna!" I told her I didn't know why I needed to leave in a rush, and she tried to hold me up. My aunt called, and I looked at the phone while the teacher tried talking to me. I said, "I must go; there's something wrong," and she proceeded to say, "What could be more important than this?" I cut her off by walking outside to answer my aunt's call. I had never heard her voice in a panic like this before, so I sprinted to my car as she told me what was happening. "I don't have a key to get inside his house; only you do. You need to leave school now! I went to the backyard by his room and heard him when I said his name, knocking on the wall, but there was no voice." She hung up to call someone who might be closer with the key.

As I made the 15-minute commute to his house into a 7-minute one, I got to the main street and turned into the entrance of the big subdivision in which he lived to see this ambulance in front of me. My heart sank with worry, and I screamed in tears, "God, let this not be for my daddy!" I tailed that ambulance, and every turn I took to get to his house, the sirens in front were going as well. They pulled up to his house, and I sank because there was already one there. With the door open, I looked around at all the neighbors that my dad had helped in the past. They were all outside, walking toward me. There were at least seven of them asking if he was alright, some from a distance, but I was too overwhelmed and shocked to answer anything from anybody.

I saw my dad come out on the stretcher, and I touched his hand, and there was a peace that I felt in what was happening to me at the time. I proceeded to ask as I got into the ambulance what happened, and he told me that there was a brain bleed and symptoms of a stroke. I sat in the ambulance with the driver, and as I frantically tried to look back at my dad, the driver stood out to me because of his calming spirit. It was a 7-minute drive, and I tried calling the pastor's wife, but there was no answer. My mom didn't answer either. I was now in the hospital, and they rushed him back. I was standing in this big hallway alone until my silence was interrupted by a phone call from the pastor's wife. I told her what was going on, but I figured she was busy. My mom then called and asked where I was. With a voice knowing she had already heard, I told her, and she said she was coming. I was alone again in the hallway, this time interrupted by a familiar face, one of my aunts. Shortly after, my dad's side of the immediate family was all there. We waited, and someone gave us a private room to sit in while waiting.

The doctor shortly after came in, and I zoned back in on, "It is a small gap of hours that a person can stay alive from experiencing this, and he was at the last hour, but it has done a lot of damage to his brain, and it is very

Have Faith?

I dropped out of high school for an extended period of time. I had a golf tournament that I needed to get out of school for, and my dad came with me, and it was so fun. It was May of 2017. After the tournament, he asked me where I wanted to go eat, and I chose sushi. He proceeded to make jokes about that being fancy, but he took me. I took pictures to commemorate the moment—well, one of many—because he took me out on dates every week, maybe twice if he picked me up from school early to spend time with him. I never really understood how my dad had 2 or 3 businesses and still had time to spend with me, but it was great knowing that he was intentional about quality time. He always made time to show generosity to people and was a deacon at our church. I loved getting out of school to go work with him because it opened my entrepreneurial mind to a different level.

The sushi was great, and we laughed and talked; he encouraged me through his words, and I was weirdly tearing up, which never happened. We proceeded to go to my grandma and his mom's house to talk, and I remembered I had a big project due tomorrow morning. I worked all night on it with my aunt and dosed off, having a little bit left to be done, but I woke up later than expected, and called my dad to tell him I needed time before he picked me up, but something was different in his voice that I couldn't pinpoint. He told me to just drive to school and that he would call to check me in. I said okay and briefly finished this project. I got in the car and started on my 20-minute commute to school, praying there was no traffic. I called my dad back to tell him that I had finished and was on the way to school, but I got no answer. I was about 4 minutes into the drive, and I was passing the exit to my dad's house to drive to school, but I had this pounding in my chest that hurt so bad, and a voice made me aware of one word, "Dad." I kept driving and calling him, but still no answer, so I sat at this nutrition spot to wait because I had to get him to call me in at school. I called a few more times again but got no answer. The pounding in my chest was getting deeper and deeper until I asked the voice, and I heard what to do, "Call your aunt," is what I heard. It just so happened that she took off work to help me finish my project, so I called her, knowing and directing her to check on my dad quickly for me because something was wrong.

I was still calling my dad, and there was still no answer. As I pulled up at the school, I heard that voice say, "Park at the nearest spot, drop the project off, and leave now!" I didn't find a parking spot at the high school, so I parked at the other building and swiftly walked in, avoiding the office ladies because of the size of the project in my hand. I proceeded to drop

3

Part Three

Breaking

Lost

Dark… An abyss
I sit and think.
Why God would you leave me here?!
I sit in this abyss & think
why am I so lost on this journey?

Lost in my thoughts that bring me back to the
beginning and ending question of Why.
Lost in my emotions that are now uncontrolled
by the tears that stream like a river.
Thinking…

You said, "I was planted by streams of your living water." ,
but yet I cry them?!
"Bringing forth fruit in every season
with leaves that never wither.",
But I feel like I'm rather withering and dead at the root.
No hope of bearing fruit, but you said,"
You would never leave me nor fail me."
You said, "you would be my strength when I am weak."
Well, I am weak, so where are YOU?!

What I didn't know then, but God knew always is this…
For something to be that reliable in every season they
have to grow roots that are seated by the living water DEEP below...
Below the surface
Before the sight of others
& in the midst of the darkness

You have to grow…. LOW in order for ME to exalt
you up from what you see as an abyss!
As you cry out to me in your weakness
I promise that I am strengthening EVERY root with no barren fruit.
Don't worry I am here and hearing you always.
Not for too much longer, joy comes in the morning.
You are never lost but instead found by Me.

Briahna Willis

Chapter 6:

Peace in Pieces

Psalms 34:18

Finally, But Suddenly!

I started to feel something with you, though. I always wanted to be friends first, but it never worked like that until I met you. Laughing, night after night of phone calls, late-night car talks, and hanging with your friends eventually turned into date after date, study nights, and you coming to practice with me often, and we were joined at the hip with marriage discussed in the future. I finally felt like someone understood me; I finally felt loved; I finally felt like I could just be myself, and no mask had to be put on around you; you just got me. You accepted all of me, as I did the same with you, while helping me progress by challenging me daily. You became a necessity in my life.

I was open with you about my past life and did not want my past habits to interrupt the forever I wanted to spend with you. It seemed too good to be true, so I distanced my heart by falling back into splitting it with commitment in mind for later. We both agreed we were just too young, and I wanted to experience more first. "If it's meant to be, it'll be," we both said. From a relationship with you to starting back talking after our time apart, it was when you texted me something that I knew would shift into our deeper next. That was until, unplanned, I saw you out one night when you were with someone, and I was too. I looked back at you, and I just watched you walk away in slow motion, and it was a feeling in my spirit of an ending in sight. I did not text you yet because I wanted you to text me first, so I waited. Days later, you texted me about the love that we had continued, and someone was over my shoulder pressuring me not to text back, so I didn't. I liked your message with a reply in mind for later.

I was up until 2:30 a.m. a few days later, struggling to go to sleep. Thoughts wondered how I was going to text you back later, and I had it in my mind, and a reasonless tear fell from my eye as I went to sleep. The reasons became clearer as I happily woke up to a knock at my door at 8:00 a.m. It was your friend standing there with no smile, no life, and no love, but just a body. She handed me her phone with a news article that read, "Girl killed in a fatal car crash," and when I asked why she woke me up to show me this, she said, "It was you." I did not believe her, so I called you for myself. Call after call, no answer after no answer—every call unanswered was the deeper my heart went into an abyss.

Now I turned around with tears filling my eyes; her friend now stood in my room, and my legs no longer felt, so I fell to the ground. I stand up to wipe my face and see what I could turn to now. I pulled out from under my bed a storage trunk of alcohol and opened a bottle of vodka in hopes of becoming numb to the pain that I felt. It did nothing but make me cry more, and I looked up and saw her friend, who sat at the foot of my bed as I tried to drink myself to sleep but woke up from knocks at my dorm room door. She became the door guard who cleaned up the empty bottles of alcohol in my room to then let familiar people only in, such as my friend, the RA, and my coach.

I couldn't close my eyes and sleep. The longer I lay, the more uncomfortable I became, so I got up and called my mom. No word came out of my mouth, but instead, tears from my soul crying out for answers were the replacement. She told me to go see a counselor, so I did. As I drove across campus with tears in my eyes, all I saw was every vision of the things we did together. I saw nothing but her everywhere. Everywhere I looked became visions of memories that we had together, but now gone forever of it happening again with her. I somehow had enough strength to make it up to the counselor's center, and as soon as I entered, my feet left from under my legs, leaving me face down again, but I had nothing to offer but tears and a cry of why to God.

I got back from the 2-hour session, and they ended up canceling the other sessions they had just for me. The door to my lone dorm room was heavily shut, and I was just going to lie down, watch something, and sleep, but I got a knock at my door from someone. I barely got the door open, and this girl pushed herself in. She was the last person I wanted to see now because they did not like each other, and now she was asking me what was happening. I told her, and she dismissed my feelings completely and replaced them with the opposite of what she had just texted me days and weeks prior. I sat defending at first and then just dismissed her from my room after going off on her.

I went to the funeral, and her best friend hugged me, but I couldn't stand to go up close, so I sat in the back to hold everything in. I glanced at an open casket with a lifeless version of you in it. As I sat in the back with an auditorium packed, flashbacks now flashed in my head about us laughing about looking good at whoever's funeral jokingly, but I did not think it would be soon.

A sleepless night tried to meet me that night, so I sat for a second in shock with no tears available. I called my friend around midnight, and she offered her room and a carpet floor to curl up on. I dozed off into a deep sleep. I woke up and met with, "AYEEEE MOEEEE!!! Never again, because why do you snore that loud?" and our laughs filled the room. She was a great friend to me, and I thank God now that He sent her into my life for that season of my life.

Morning After Mourning!

My mom asked me to drop some Sprite and some medicine off to my uncle. I loved talking to him, and he was goofy. I called him and was met with coughing on the phone, one that I had never heard from him before, so I prayed for him quickly and then proceeded to ask if he needed anything else from the store. He said, "Nah, I'm good; just hurry over with the Sprite and medicine." I responded with, "Ard, BYEEEE!" He came to let me in and rushed back to the room to lie down. We talked briefly because he didn't want me to get whatever it was. I asked him, "Did you get tested for COVID unc?" He replied with coughs of "yes, still waiting for the results." I then told him, "I love you and will see you soon when you feel better. Call me if you need anything else!" He responded, "I will, and I love you too." Shortly after I left his house, I got a call from my mom saying that he had COVID, and because I did not wear a mask, I needed to get tested. I went, and the results were negative. He went to the hospital shortly after and battled COVID for a month before he passed away. I sat in this big service, so confused as to why anything could come from this. WHY and HOW were the only questions that circled my mind, so I found things to do to occupy it with taking my cousin's pictures.

A few weeks later, I drove to Texas, separate from my mom, aunt, and granny, to see my cuzzos (cousins). I arrived later in the day, and by the time I got there, I saw all my little cousins except one; he went out with friends. I took the other three with me because they wanted to go to TopGolf with me so I could teach them. My bro from college was in the area too, so I asked if he wanted to slide; he came with us, and it was a fun night. I wish the oldest one would've come through, too; I know we had our differences, but I loved him and wanted him to come.

Growing up and with him being around often in Arkansas, I took advantage of that time because he was the only one closest to me in age. I didn't know what it was like to have siblings closer in age, so I loved being a 'big sister.' We were so different from each other, and it clashed sometimes; he liked video games, and I liked sports. The advice I gave him was because I loved him and didn't want him to go through things like me, but especially because he was a young Black man. I wanted him to be aware of things that I was taught. I would check in on social media because I saw the Instagram lives that he sent me. It almost felt like every day, sometimes more.

Whenever he was in the city, my aunt called and told me to pick him up and hang out, so I did, lol. I entered the house, greeting him by saying, "Watsup? Get a fit together because one of us can't be looking dusty." He laughed and put on another outfit, and we left on the journey in the city, talking about life. The drives consisted of sometimes him asking funny questions regarding life and the importance of having good friends, so I answered if I knew.

As we were still in Texas, my mom was talking about how tall he was now, and I had not seen him before I left, so I had hopes of coming soon to see him.

A few nights after returning, I was with my niece, looked at my phone, and saw a live notification from him. I heard a voice say, "Click on it," but I said I would wait for a minute and ended up forgetting to go back to it. That night, I was sitting with my niece, waiting for her to go to sleep, and I saw over three missed calls from my mom. I called her back to hear her voice cracking, saying, "They shot him, and I need to pray and fast until the surgery is over," so I headed back home, praying on the road for God to perform a miracle on my baby cousin like He did before for my other cousin. I got home and asked my mom what happened, and she told me what she knew. As she told me, I felt anger consume me every minute following because he was such a good hearted dude and was changing in life for the better.

I prayed in the shower for a miracle, and while getting out of the shower with my first foot hitting the cold ground and the water now turning off, I heard my mother whaling from her soul for the second time in that month. I felt this cold ground consuming my feet; a rage-like venom was rushing through my body with this anger. I quickly put clothes on to comfort her, even with me being in pieces for the hate-filled act that was just done to my baby cousin. "How could this happen, days before Easter, really, God? A day that people celebrate the day that Jesus died a gruesome death for us, yet someone else that I love dying a gruesome death! Why God!? He was a little lamb that shouldn't have been slain, WHY would you do this?!" I said to God in anger and confusion. I slowly became numb.

I sat in my room after my momma was lying down and I curled up in a ball of weakness and tears to muster words to sing, "You sustain, You sustain; in the middle of it all, You remain the same; through the rain, still you reign, You sustain."

As the last words of God being my sustainer were released from my mouth, a blanket of His peace covered me.

It was as if the anger in my heart toward that boy who murdered him had vanished, and I had a calm sense of peace that was unexplainable. I went up to Texas for the next few days and was silent, but I also did not have the right words to say to those around me because what I experienced was unexplainable then.

Chapter 7:

Trauma & Forgiveness

Church Trauma!

Matthew 6
Matthew 7:3-5

In college, my loving teammate and her boyfriend, now husband, invited me to go to church for the hundredth time, and I finally went expecting something. I just lost what I believed to be the love of my life, and I wanted answers from God. I was expected to receive a word, which I did, and I quickly forgot because of the trauma afterward. I went to the front after they left to get prayer and received more trauma, but irritation with my hands raised like instructed by the woman standing in front of me with eyes that I have seen so many times before, judgment. After I asked for prayer for grief, she proceeded to say, "Mhmmm, I sense a homosexual spirit inside of you." She asks someone for the oil and takes a boatload, drenching my face and pushing me to the ground. That Jawn really hurt y'all; I woke up with bumps, bruises, and pimples the next morning.

This really tore my heart even more because at that time, as the bumps, bruises, and pimples physically went away, they still remained seeping in deeper internally.

The peace that I wanted to grow from being in a church was now scattered in pieces! The one place that I felt should have given me that peace was now a place that brought me to not attend. When I did pop my head in from time to time during that season, all that I saw was the judgment in their eyes. It made me then wonder why the only people who looked like Jesus were my loving teammate and her boyfriend, and why these people traumatized me. The church leaders had pride internally displayed in their hearts that I saw, yet I had eyes on me for displaying it in a more outward way. I didn't understand then, but now I do.

Facing the Smoke

I sat there, facing the smoke I wanted to deal with; both were poison that would either hide me deeper or bring poison to someone. Do I allow him to tell on me, or do I give him what he doesn't need? I chose myself the first time until I saw the result start to corrode his body from what I knew him to be before. At this time, I was 17 with a girlfriend who was with me because it was summer.

I valued a deeper relationship with one of my brothers and my mom. I was willing to do anything to have that by all means. I started telling the one brother how I just got a girlfriend and how I was gay. What I thought were good conversations were really masked by something deeper that I did not notice. The "Can you drop me off here?" and "Take me right here quickly" were cool, but now my eyes were open to seeing these dark locations that I had never been to before. Yes after yes was given, and I started noticing his smaller body actions changed in the process of every yes that I accepted. I was busy with my girlfriend about to go to a park, and I got a call from him urgently needing me to pick someone up. I explained I was busy, but he proceeded to blackmail me because he met the girl. He says, "If you don't do this for me, then I will tell momma you are gay." I sat in disbelief, so I said OKAY a few more times because I didn't want her to know.

He sent me the address to the location, and it was only 3 minutes away from my grandma's but closer to where the gunshots came from at night. I pulled up, and it was very familiar, like I had seen this house in the past. Then I remembered that the last girl I was with took me like it was a museum and said, "This is the crack house." I was so confused in the driveway, but I told the girl to get the knife, and I had a Taser. He said to pick one person up, but there was instead one woman and a grown man who was at least twice our age now inside the backseat of my car. I drove there as fast as possible because what did I just say yes to? We got inside his room, and they were chilling, but the girl I was with quickly pulled me out of the room to go outside. "Bri, do you not see what your brother is getting into?" I really didn't know then, so I let her tell me, and I wanted to go see for myself. By the time I got back to his room, the man was blocking the door from me by saying, "Your brother is just sleeping right now," and it looked like he was sleeping on the bed, but I saw the objects in the distance that the girl I was with described and what they were.

It hurt so bad to see him like this. I had a golf tournament out of town that I wanted him to take me to, and he promised he would, but the day of, I said no to getting drugs this time for him, and he started yelling at me. I cried and drove to my other brother, crying in his arms, to ask if he could take me to a golf tournament, and he canceled everything, packed a bag, and took me.

Just recently, I asked God to reveal any unforgiveness toward people, and I remembered this as soon as I woke up. God said in the dream, "FORGIVE YOUR BROTHER!" As soon as I woke up from my dream, he was at the front door, and I pulled him aside and told him that I had forgiven him.

I promise that if you ask God where, what, or who, He will surely let you know.

Failure to Forgive.

Hosting bitterness inside and staying angry is like drinking poison for the unforgiveness that you have toward people, but you expect them to feel the side effects when it's really you sinking yourself lower and lower into the unforgiveness dwelling in your heart. For so long, I had been taking shots of poison from everything said and done to me, yet not expressing anything because my words had been trampled on in the past. I didn't forgive people a lot of the time, and I wondered why so much anger had the ability to consume me. I used to be so furious, with rage overtaking me to the point of finding myself starting to shake and my eyes changing colors. I just thought that was normal for so long, but little did I know it was deeper.

I threw my phone at this girl because she continued to call me mentally unstable for crying and expressing my feelings. The first time, I was quiet, even though she caught me cutting a pineapple with a chef's knife in one hand when saying it. I saw what I could do with this feeling boiling up inside of me, but my friend from college told me not to entertain her because there was no point. I get back in the room to find myself shaking and my eyes now a different color, and that is when I figured out that this was something else.

I was at a golf tournament, and they canceled the rest of the days due to rain, so I got to stay in the hotel room another night, so I got some alcohol. Prior to that, I asked if anyone could switchrooms because I knew I did not need to stay with this same girl, but everyone said my snoring was too loud, so I was left with her. I was tipsy now, and I was talking to one of the boys, and she interrupted our conversation of laughter with defense of him in mind, only hearing a portion of the conversation. She said the same words as days prior, and I threw my phone and other things close to me at her, though I missed, and then I lunged at her. In mid-air, I was snatched by one of the boys, and he carried me out screaming and in rage, ready to fight, but my loving teammate and friend at the time found a way to calm me down by the ocean. All of that retaliation had to have a seed to produce this outcome.

When you stay quiet for so long because you are comfortable with things being said regarding your mental well-being and intellectual level without correction, it reaps a harvest.

Starting now, I had to choose to start speaking up by informing people that this is not my portion, and I will not let anyone speak a word curse over my life, no matter how small it seems to others. We must show people how to treat us, especially when we are born again, but in a nice and righteous way, of course.

If anyone has said anything negative about your life through negative words or even your names that were born from a place of pain, I cancel anything that was spoken negatively against you and/or your destiny; it is null and void right now, and I uproot it in Jesus' mighty name!

Forgive Me.

2 Corinthians 12:9

For everything that has ever happened to me or that I have done to someone else, I need to forgive myself first.

Unforgiveness in the heart is what holds people captive from being free for themselves.

If you are choosing to hold on for yourself, it is saying that you don't trust that vengeance is the Lord's. Yes, they did those things to you when you were younger, or they spoke bad things about you, but you don't even have to worry; instead (1 Peter 5:7), "Cast all your cares on Him, for He cares for you."

When I failed to forgive people for the words they had spoken over me or maybe their actions, I started to have unforgiveness in my heart. In order to live a life that is truly free, I had to forgive everybody that I even remembered and any bit of anger started to rise. I had to forgive myself first. Your failure to forgive can hold you back from so many breakthroughs. No matter what that person did to you in the past, even though it may be hard, it is now your responsibility to forgive them. The only way you can find the strength to forgive is in your weakness, which is only rooted in God.

For you to not continue to take shots of poison from them every time you think about them or maybe see them, you need to forgive them by forgiving yourself first. Casting your cares on Him looks like you just talking to God and telling Him how that hurt you, and I am breaking ties with the spirit of unforgiveness right now! If you know that you have some people that you need to forgive, fill in the blank as you pray this for every person that you need to forgive.

FORGIVE YOU FIRST: I forgive myself for _____ happening to me.

FORGIVE THEM: "God, I forgive _____ for _____."

I will recommend this source below because it has and is helping me currently. **Unoffendable by Brant Hansen**

Chapter 8:
Strapped Down

Applause and Praises

I sat in the middle of a very loud environment of applause and praises, which some may think of as an accomplishment. I sat there with my hands in motion to respond to a dap from my bros from what was said, but I was confused as to why I got this praise and applause for something that was opposite of what I really wanted: love. From an early age, I always hung out with dudes before I was labeled and known as a stud (the masculine girl in relationships), but now, more than ever, in that season, I had bros in college. I was mixed with emotions going to a college that was 20 hours away and worried about how I would meet people, but I had that on lock! I did some research and chose to post my #UMES around the time I signed there. I told a little bit about myself, and I immediately received more text messages from a lot of girls. I instantly started making connections with some of the other studs, as they were all upperclassmen, putting me on game. They added me to their group chats, and I started school in the summer by reading what looked like another language with this DMV slang that I was confused about immediately because, for the longest weeks, I could not find out who "Moe" was lol. (It just means, "Bro.")

I got more texts from girls, and I started to think one was odd because it was not a liking but more of wanting to be friends. It was weird because I never had girls like friends, and this girl that I talked about in "Finally, But Suddenly" was trying to be friends, nothing more?! This was a challenge that was activated. I established a rule that I would not mess with or talk to anyone in golf in that way, so they were automatic friends in my book. The closest to me maintaining a friendship, I was around 17 and was about to start living a "Thot Stud Summer" lol. I had my friends with me more so at this time, and one was close because we played summer softball for years together and lived down the street from each other, too. She introduced me to her girlfriend, and we became cool. Meanwhile, my dad was still in rehab, but I was sad because he was not the same as before, so I found ways to leave the hospital. I suppressed my feelings and words more by going to weed and attempting that Thot Stud Summer with girls, and I found both, but one was made singular, a girl. I got into a relationship with this very sweet girl who was cool, and I would come over as her mom cooked Jamaican patties, and whew child, they were so good! I introduced my girlfriend at the time to my best friend, and they just immediately clicked, and we all started to hang out as couples.

One day, I was so excited to go home because I ordered a new strap-on for me to use because she was a virgin. I told my friend to hurry up when I got her from school because I had places to be, and she knew what that meant, but she asked with understanding anyway. I told her exactly why, and she asked to see it as we were in the house, and it was now like a new one after that day, but used after that moment of her pushing on me sexually. I felt so bad, and I continued, and we said we wouldn't say anything to each other's partners until I was with her girl and got so drunk. She asked the right questions, and I freely answered. A few days later, I was leaving this golf tournament that I had won to a disruption by a group chat with the four of them, saying that we had cheated, so I asked the driver, my brother, what

I should do, and he told me to lie. "Did anyone see you? Did anyone record anything? Okay, there is no proof." I was so uneasy doing it, but doing this over text messages was easy. I asked him if we could stop by her house since we would pass through, and he took me over there and waited in the car for me. I walked up the stairs to see her sister, that I heard of, but never seen before now opening the door for me, and I looked on the ground to see plastic covering the majority of it in the living room walkway. She pointed for me to go into her room, and it was weird, but I did.

I walked in, seeing way more plastic laid out on the ground, and asked as I was about to kiss her, "Babe, what kind of things are y'all about to do with the place?" Silence filled the room, and I was confused. She looked at me with now different eyes as she pulled out the biggest knife that I have ever seen before, but now that was pressed against my throat gently. Now I was met with a thick foreign accent that was now consuming her speech, by saying, "Nothing will be done if you are honest with me." So, I prepared my body language to lie because I knew I needed to if I planned to survive. I walked closer to the door in fear, with the aim of leaving, and she put the knife by her face like a toy and said in a different voice, "I wouldn't try that if I were you {with an evil laugh}. I will throw this knife, hit an artery in your neck, and watch you bleed out on this floor. And just in case I do miss, my sister knows what to do {another evil laugh}. Answer my question, Bri, because you are making this harder than it must be. I have a gun as well; if you would rather me go that route…" I was sitting there with a little part of this toxic attraction in me, enjoying this, but I also had fear and wanted to get out of this situation, and how I proceeded was very important and required me to be cautious. I thought to myself as this foreign voice was speaking to me in the form of her, and the only thought in my mind was, "I have to put on a stellar performance to get myself out of this one."

She began to reach over toward the gun now in my sight that was peeking out of the pillow, and I ran up to her and asked her, "Why would you think I would do that to you? I don't understand why you would believe I could do that to you because I love you." Tears started to roll down my face, and I told her that I would not do that to her. It was almost as if someone snapped there fingers and her being sweet was activated again, she asked me questions about the state that she was just in. After that, we hugged, and she came down to meet my brother. I observed her the whole time she talked to him, and it was the weirdest thing I have ever seen, because didn't you almost kill me? Now, you are over here acting like nothing happened and dapping my brother up. WHAT THE HECK?

She went back upstairs, and I couldn't tell him what just happened with the knife and gun because he is a very passionate brother who would not let that fly, so I sat there for a second, processing this interaction. I finally shared with him that she was mad and ended up being okay after I lied to her about it, and he praised me for it as I sat in a lot of deep thought. I get applauded and praised for telling lies? This was the foundation of the other things moving forward because this idea of praise was established through a lie in the first place. Things will not stand for long if the foundation is not stable.

I was in college, back in Maryland, after I took my COVID year off for golf. I was back on the scene this time with a plan in mind of selling jungle juice on campus. On my first day out, I pulled up, and I again had never met a stranger, especially when I was under the influence, so I went up to this group of girls and asked if they needed some juice; they bought some and got another. I got my customers' numbers, but I was happy to have one specifically. I gradually texted her to see where it would go. I walked up to another group of girls, and these were the ones that I knew I hit the jackpot because my gay meter WENT OFF, but I kept it business, even though I noticed their eyes.

At the other parties, I went with my bros, and they helped me sell the drinks as well. The campus security shut down one party, and we packed up quickly to head to another, but I saw that group of girls from earlier without rides, so there were 7 or 8 of them in my hatchback. A whole basketball team came out of my car, and my bros met me over there, and all of them were trying to smack on this one girl at the same time. She was a pretty girl on campus who a lot of people wanted. She got out of my car with her best friend, and they were both flirting with me. My bro interrupted, and I gave him that look, but they just ignored him and kept talking, and eventually, one of those two came back with me.

"Ayoooooo!!! Moeee!!! You are really that n**** Bri! How did you... Never mind, we all know (laughs)!" Things like this happened often and were what I was applauded for when, so many times, I wanted to offer that girl more than pleasure to the body but yearned to have someone love me as the girl previously talked about in "Finally, But Suddenly" did. I took pride in the sex I offered because that is where my praise was given when I was rarely able to receive anything. This is a thing in which I made a god: sex. A different girl every day, week, or month, maybe two or three; shoot, I don't know, I was "free" to do whatever with whoever. I then started to view myself as an idol, as I had finally been given something—praise and applause.

Sex offered me the ability to replace silence in my lack of vulnerability to feelings and instead gave me a way to let out aggression in a way to prove my point and my position.

I tried to prove myself and my point in the wrong way because I replaced it with a counterfeit way.

After a few relationships went by of me trying to give someone my heart, they repaid me with cheating or me not fitting in the confounds of the label. After this, I needed time without any type of commitment to someone, but the objective was to be able to conquer someone, sometimes using my mouth to manipulate the perfect lie to get what I wanted. I used to love the challenge of being with a virgin; to me, it was a game played and won by me multiple times.

Back then, after she passed away, girls were just bodies to me, and with most girls that I pursued aimlessly after, I had only one goal in mind, fill this empty void again. The problem with this is that people are not just bodies to be conquered for my personal gain; people are sacred temples. I did not care to understand that then because I enjoyed pleasing myself so much that I did not even realize that I went into a lot of sacred places.

Trapped in Freedom

Why did I feel like a slave to these things that people labeled as "Freedom"? I was going through the motions that I was so used to with another girl, but this time, I felt empty and like no matter what, I would not be satisfied. I had never felt this way before, so I just thought maybe it was the girl, so I dropped one off and called the other girl to come over. Nothing changed, and I had the same feelings of not being satisfied. I dropped the other girl off and picked up another from the same dorm that same day. I noticed they knew each other's name because they said "hey" to each other in passing, but that was it, so I thought nothing else.

Why did I feel like a slave to money? I had the bread but was at a high risk of losing my freedom. I was free financially to do what I wanted, but all at the price of hustling and looking behind my back and almost getting arrested. That is not living free, but instead living financially bound. Was this just a foreshadowing of what would come if I continued making money this way? Almost.

I woke up on a peaceful morning with my sights set on picking up my mom and aunt from the airport after a great weekend of selling juice on campus. I was now sitting up on my bed with a backwood that I rolled because I had to spark up before they came over. I was now just sitting there enjoying my last blunt with me, myself, and I before I couldn't for the next week because I had a golf tournament, and they were in town. After I finished, I got up from my comfortable bed, opened the sliding door and windows, and took a shower. I finally looked at my phone and received 7 missed phone calls from this number that I did not save and texts that were from the same person with familiarity with these text messages. I waited until I got on my 2.5-hour drive to the airport to make the call.

Panic filled my phone regarding the fact that I couldn't put words to the FaceTime call. "Bri!!! You need to stop selling your juice now! I am at the hospital right now, and they rushed her and two others in after drinking your juice. Right before the ambulance came into the room, I took up the bottle and threw it out, but I don't know about the other people. The campus security is working with the police to find out stuff, so you need to stop and lay low!" I immediately started asking, "Is she okay? What happened? What did the doctor say?" The doctor came in, and she rushed me off the phone with, "I will call you back!"

I sat in the car on this long ride that I was now 30 minutes into, and all I heard was, "Get them to throw everything away now!" Immediately, I called all my bros, telling them what was going on, and they responded, saying, "Dang! What the *bro, what do you need from us? We gotchu fam." I proceeded to ask if they could pull up to my crib and do what this voice just told me. I made calls for them to get over there, and they facetimed me while they did it. It hurt so bad to see the new bottles and products I had just restocked go to the trash, but I had no other choice if I had a chance of surviving this.

I got back on the road of silence, and I was overwhelmed with worry consuming my every thought, so an hour later, I called the girl back. She was much calmer, but the first words earlier still flowed and echoed in my soul, saying, "Bri!!! You need to stop selling your juice, bro!" I then asked her what the doctor said, and she said, "It was an allergic reaction; she is allergic to pineapples." So many thoughts filled my mind because I asked everyone if they had food allergies, and I remembered her, and the other people said no because I had other options and knew my customers who were allergic to certain fruits. I proceeded to say, "I asked everyone if they were allergic to anything, and they said no, but let me talk to her sis." She handed her the phone, and I said, "I'm sorry, sis," and calmly, she said, "You are good; I forgot to tell you." Her friend grabbed the phone back because she wasn't supposed to be talking that much or something and told me for the third time, "Bri!!! You need to stop selling your juice; you are a cool person and have a lot going for yourself; please just look out for yourself." I listened and then told her, "Okay, bye," as I was now 30 minutes away from the airport, and the only thing on my mind was those other two people.

This voice that spoke earlier now said, "Tell them what is going on as soon as they get in the car." I said, "What? Are you crazy?" and in a calmer tone, the voice repeated, "Tell them what is going on as soon as they get in the car," so I did. I greeted my mom and my aunt, and when they got into the car, they saw my face, and I told them what happened. I could feel the disappointment in the air, and they just said I needed to figure it out and that I should have put ingredients on the bottles. We then went to Nando's in DC to pick up some food before our dreadful 2.5-hour drive to my apartment.

Strapped Down

Romans 7:15-20

My aunt and mom dropped me off at the team bus to travel for my golf tournament about 30 minutes away in Ocean City. The next morning, I sat in the van early in the morning and headed to our morning round, but we had an option to stay in the van because of the 2-hour gap, so we did. They informed us that we had to go back to the hotel because the other team's bus had broken down, and I wanted to talk to whoever it was. I was familiar with their coach and a few players, so I talked. The one I was cool with was not there, but I could tell that her other teammate and friend was willing to talk with me as I saw an interest in her eyes. So, I proceeded to ask little questions, but the conversation ended because my aunt and mom had my car and I wanted to know where they were. "Hey mommy, where are y'all?" "We had a little issue with your tire, so we are getting it repaired right now." I said OKAY and hung up, but something told me that was not all and to call my aunt because she would keep it real, so I did. "Hey, what happened?" She walked away from my mom and continued the conversation by saying, "I don't know who you were messing with, but someone slashed your tire, Bri." I loudly said on the bus, "WHAT?! Someone slashed my *** tire!?" My focus was now everywhere else, but it was this last round that I had to play.

I got done with the round and went with my mom in my car instead of with the team. I walked up to my car and saw this doughnut tire, and immediately, rage filled my mind about who would do this, and it clicked.

The altercation at my crib with a girl and friends pulling up on me because I messed with her and someone that I didn't know was her friend. All those thoughts of pointing fingers immediately stopped playing in my head and were replaced with what I was going to do when I got the new tire and dropped my mom off. I got those tasks done and called my plug to cop some weed. After getting some and leaving, I went to my favorite store in the city the college was in to get some snacks and a pack of backwoods. Soon after talking to him and his little daughter, I get back to the crib to roll the joint and then take a shower, and I had already planned on turning my phone off to sit in and watch movies for the rest of the night.

So, I was on the bed, now laid out in my college dorm room, in silence with the smoke consuming the air, along with another breath God gave me, and deciding to give it to this blunt. At that moment, I was strapped to the bed that I once found comfort in, and I became a conduit of vision with everything that has happened in my life—the things I have told you and not—now flowing like a movie through my head. God, in that moment, showed me all the things that he saved me from from another perspective. For the shooting toward the car, He showed His mighty hand hovering over me and my dad's car. For me trying to attempt suicide in the car going 120 mph and steering in the direction of the woods, He displayed a supernatural boundary and guardrail that were placed by Him to protect me. For my "friend," who pointed the gun at me jokingly, He showed me his hand, blocking the trigger from being touched. For my mind, which was jumbled from manipulation and a lot of mind games, He showed me that He was a mind regulator. For the diagnosis that I received of bipolar disorder and ADHD, He showed me that I am loved and am not the label that was tried to be placed on me by the world, but instead an overcomer. For the girl who was about to kill me for cheating on her, He showed that He was my great Protector. For all the girls that I had messed with and some that have not been the same since, He showed me His daily infinite mercy and grace. At that moment, I heard, who I then knew was Him say, "Briahna, are you done trying to live life your way because if you continue, you will die!" I chose at that moment not to waste away my life voluntarily but instead to give up and give Him a chance, ALL IN.

A few months after that day, I decided to start the process of giving these things up fully, but I still found myself drinking, smoking, and still entertaining the idea of another girl. I tried stopping on my own strength asking God to "pray the gay away", but all it did was leave me feeling that God wasn't there after my encounters with Him. I then started praying that God would give me revelation on why I still had a desire for messing with girls, smoking, drinking, etc., and I believe my loving teammate sent me a sermon on Sunday to watch. I wanted to stop all these things and overcome them, but I did not understand why I still found myself doing the things sometimes that I knew I should not do because I knew God did not like them. I sat there, and God really encountered me again and told me that **"this journey will be challenging but rewarding,"** so that day, I sat in my room in awe of God speaking so much more, and then, with understanding, I officially said "yes" to Him.

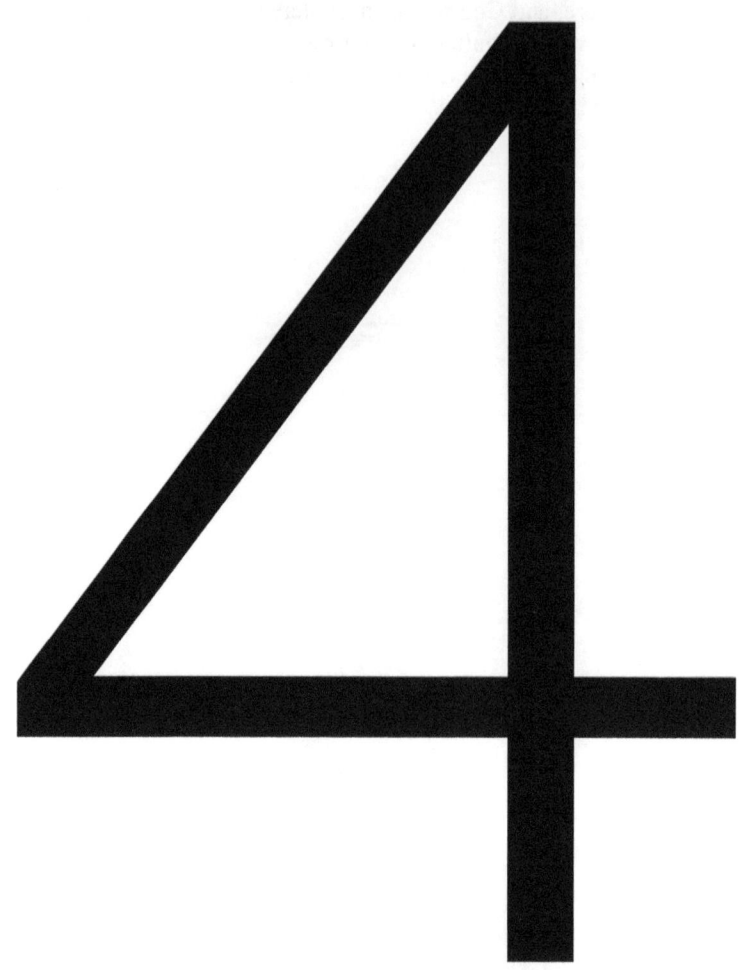

Part Four

Refiner/
Refining

Ask and You will receive...Your heart back.

1. Numbing

You are trying to protect yourself from pain.

I used to be under... under Anesthesia the world gave me. She numbed me from feeling the things that truly hurt me, and told me, "You aren't playing your role, so Numb your feelings."

2. Stealing

The presence of Anesthesia Snatched the feelings inside of the conscious state that I once dwelled in. So, I went under fully into the world, to fill a heart that was stolen.

3. Finding

Fully finding a mask to wear to remain numb because this is what was now comfort to my soul that she had me under.
After gaining a blurry view of what is seen ahead, I Realized that these Real Eyes are now showing me these Real Lies. Awake now.

4. Painful

When you see the state that this leaves you in, Confusion enters your body and the first thing you wake to is a desperate thirst for truth, way, and life. Instead, you turn to a truth that seems accurate, a way that seems pleasing to "your spirit", and life worth living alone.

5. Feeling

is what needs to take place for the Filler to come into the place that was full of substances to then

6. Detox

that empty place. He wants to be the

7. Mediator

of my soul. A keeper of my heart, soul, and a mind

8. Mender.

Every touch like a supernatural stitch bringing places that were open for His surgery to take place, drawn together with His love through His children to reveal THE TRUTH, THE WAY, and THE LIFE. That only comes from seeking Him, through searching daily, and taking you to His plan for your life.

A Touch from Heaven.

-Briahna Willis

Chapter 9:

Feel to Be Filled

Malachi 3:2-3

Feel to Be Filled (Journal entry)

I feel nothing. Everything that is going on makes me want to go back to the things that once satisfied my soul and diminished my spirit. I feel like a zombie going on in this season from numbly talking about grief, being healed, seeing miracles, witnessing deliverance, and continually encouraging people. I do and see all of this because God showed and told me to, but it still feels alone, desolate, and isolated here. No matter how many days I cry myself to sleep from those suicidal thoughts trying to overtake me, a small feeling of peace still subsides here. I really feel small. I feel like God is not even a big God, like everyone says right now. I cry, but you are not here to heal me. I am hurting, and my soul is whaling through a cry that feels like it's been left unheard. My voice felt like an echo in the wind. My mourning of the old me sometimes holds me back from experiencing the new thing that God showed me because of the bondage that was once so familiar. Familiarity and comfort are the things that keep me in chains. Seeing something from the past that once brought me comfort instead of moving forward into the next, and even though I may feel alone, I have to muster the strength to walk deeper with the Comforter. I must keep going because I see that prison that once kept me stagnant and unfilled when God wants to fill me with and keep me in perfect peace. **I know that peace is free, but it costs so much to lose it.**

When I awake from the tears that drowned my bed and floor and after crying out to God about my feelings, I wake up in the morning from the mourning of yesterday renewed because I chose not to give it to myself or others but instead to God. Moving forward is easy when you no longer hold on because of the decision that you made to ask God to be your Wonderful Counselor and Prince of Peace. I'd rather He invade me fully to constantly be the Ruler of these prideful ways of mine. I'd rather not a wondering person, myself, be counseled by my feelings yet still being a peasant of my own pieces left scattered.

I need Him to sustain me instead of trying to further stain me.

I need Him to be my Lord instead of my being lord of my own life. When I cry and go for alcohol, drugs, pills, or girls, it always brings me closer to what I thought I wanted, and, in the end, I was starting from the start again. Race after race because every time I went to those things, I always ended back at the starting line instead of running with no journey in mind with someone who knows me better than I know myself. I need to wake up to God being there for me because I will always leave myself going back for more. **The Filler will come in when you decide to feel.**

Open Heart Surgery.

John 15:19

Surgery is not a thing that does not stay clean because the surgeon must cut you and open certain areas to reach other areas that are intricately located internally.

> **In this process, it will not always be peaches and cream, but it requires you to hold on and have faith in the outcome that you may not see yet.**

That would be a bad surgery if someone does not understand what they are doing fully, but be encouraged because you have the best surgeon who knows every vessel and vein in your body specifically because He made it! I promise that the surgery will not end in failure. I know because I have come out on the other side of a lot of surgeries that the same surgeon has performed on me. When I thought I needed eye surgery, He knew I needed heart surgery because of the insecurities attached.

Just admit that you do not know everything. I promise it is okay to admit that you don't, but you haven't. You have held yourself from being exalted, and this exaltation only comes through admission that you need help and you don't know everything. Now, your heart has become hard because people, for a long time, have not listened to the knowledge that God placed on the inside of you from an early age.

When you ask for God to replace a callused and hard heart with a clean heart of flesh again, He will restore that in you. Not even AI knows the amount of hair on your head or what you will do before they even manifest in the physical realm. You are so focused on the things that make sense in your own understanding of the purpose of life and why we were created, and you choose to trust yourself. You fail to admit that you are an unstable foundation alone. I understand that you want to be heard and understood by people, but the truth is that if you are following the Truth, things will not always make sense, and you will be misunderstood. The beauty of that is it will bring you so much wisdom that is not your own, but only when you finally admit that you do not understand everything. Accept the open heart surgery from the top surgeon EVER!

Ask for Your Heart Back

When God shows you a vision for something that requires a lot of faith and can cause more worry, we can give that situation to our hearts. Instead of giving it to God to mold and shape in time, we go to the easy option: the world. We then find ourselves asking people to help by getting other opinions instead of asking the One who created them to think.

> **We worry about how things will work for our good instead of how they will always work together for the good of those who love God.**

We consume our minds with emotions, worry, and the future, even though it is not our burden to carry.

All this consumption around the heart because of mixing two things that were never meant to be, culture of the world opposed to The Kingdom, it will cloud our judgment. We can allow the things that culture puts on us to cloud our overall vision that God is trying to give to us in this season. True clarity in The Kingdom way has a first step. You have to ask God for your heart back. Just like you have to be born to be born again, a restored heart comes with this new life too. Pieces of the old heart were stripped away because of the mere presence of culture, consuming every worry and vision. Asking God for our hearts back is asking God for the pieces of you that the culture has once rather, unknowingly, or knowingly stole your innocence, your heart, and/or your childhood from you. The devil stole it because he knows if he can cloud you with doubt in yourself, fear of purpose and vision, keep you bitter towards people, and cause confusion, he wins.

Say this as a sign of being aware and fully surrendered: "God, I cannot and will not allow for the worry and confusion to lead me; I need my heart back fully in order to give everything to You completely." This is the true first step. I'm so lit for you! What's the point of giving something that you do not have? Asking for your heart back symbolizes that you are willing to gain back the pieces of you that have been given to culture. You are declaring to God in the act of faith because He wants you to ask and receive WHOLE HEARTEDLY (Jeremiah 29:13). On the other hand, He can also not be moving in our timing because our heart posture is not correct. Coming to God, He wants our intentions with what we offer to be pleasing to Him in order for them to align with His good and perfect will for our lives. He cannot give you more of something if you do not have the intent to steward things well. I encourage you to not just ask Him for your heart back, but do it with the intention of doing what He wants you to do.

If we come to Him asking for our hearts fully, we can grow through things that God needs us to go through first. We hold on to the past because that is what we are familiar with, but what if God was trying to leave that in the past for a reason? What if we are seeing things through the vision of culture and what was invested there instead of looking from the heart of the Kingdom of Heaven? God wants us to know that "His ways are higher than our own," but yet we are consumed by vision received from a place of half-heartedness. Since God is the Filler of everything, why are we not able to bring even the major surgeries to Him? Will you be so scared to be cut that you forget the extraction of the cancer cells of the world that the surgeon now needs to remove from you? He wants us to give Him our whole heart because that is what He looks at, and if you are unable to do that, He is the God that mends every broken heart. He is the One who restores more than what the world has taken from you. Ask Him for your whole heart back, so that you can now seek Him with the same heart that He is ready to give you and mend. If you ask for it and it is in alignment with His will being done through you, you will receive it.

Replace the Whole Thing!

John 14:30

Romans 8:28

When things heat up in life, what do you allow to pour out? Is it pure or toxic? Imagine having an older coffee maker—not the Keurig, but instead, the things before that, which required you to have coffee filters. Ground coffee is the substance that you put in the filter to produce, with the water, your result, the coffee. Imagine you are in a grocery store and know that on this fun adventure, you need to buy some more ground coffee to make the best coffee ever! You walk into the coffee and tea aisle and know you want salted caramel flavor, but you see that the dark roast is cheaper. Will you settle for more that is cheap and low in quality, or will you pay a little bit more for quality?

The cheap dark roast ground coffee represents the version the devil has manufactured, with different flavors becoming the vices in this world and culture to consume daily.

This product is something that makes you keep having to get more than one cup daily because it seemed like it was so much more, but now you need more. Each sip of this coffee produced represents all the vices that people go to and the ones that I once went to drink cups or maybe even gallons of daily, such as alcohol, weed, pills, lean, relationships, manipulation, sex, etc. It seemed so good because I had trained my body to only drink things from this manufacturer. This coffee that is producing the counterfeit may seem to be better, but it caused more internal damage to my soul, heart, and spirit than I knew because some of these addictive ingredients were hidden.

What I didn't know is that, as I was consuming these products so often, it really gave me a callused heart where some pieces were taken, my soul was imprisoned, and the Spirit was mourning within me.

This product is sold more often because it looks like the right thing to get when people do not know the value that is already inside of them, so they sell and imprison their soul with the counterfeit. This product is always available near you and often restocked by the manufacturer, the devil, because it requires you to keep coming back for more. The more you stay in the cycle of thinking you are the god of your own actions, the more you continue to think that your life is your own, and the more you think that you can do this life without God, is the very moment you continue to buy more of this product.

We live in a sinful world and culture that will produce something that is sometimes coffee that tastes good, but something that you have to have more of. So many of us will settle for the cheap version of ground coffee every day in our lives when God has already paid for the expensive one for us. Yes, it will require more of you, and you will have to detox from the old things you once knew to be "right," but it will be worth it in the end, I promise. We no longer settle for the off-brand version or the counterfeit when God wants us to experience the real thing, which will be better for our health in the end. I refuse to settle for some cheap coffee when my Father has all the resources that I need that are in His will for my eternal life and salvation. Because you have settled for the cheap version for so long, your body does not know how to drink the authentic version originally meant for you.

You need a detox. The counterfeit will not be beneficial for where God is trying to take you.

I was living a religious, church-cultured life; it was the cheap ground coffee placed in that filter. When I was living my life smoking, drinking, manipulating people, having sex with a lot of girls, and more, I was drinking the cheap ground coffee that the manufacturer gave me, often knowing that I would have to continue going back day after day for more. Even though I was drinking that cheap ground coffee, God was gracious and merciful enough when He poured His living water in.

    I chose to replace the whole off-brand ground coffee with the quality I was meant to drink because I know the quality of what comes out now will be way better for me in the long run. So many times, God can speak to His children, and you can receive Him in a way that you will know Him to be at that very time of your life. When I was in the world, living what I thought was my best life, He told me not to mess with certain girls, and though I did not understand, He spoke and poured even through me choosing the counterfeit daily, and I listened.

Do not allow anyone to tell you that "God would never speak to you in that way," because He can do anything to meet you right where you are because He is Limitless.

There are steps that you take on this journey, and sometimes, He has to test your seed of obedience with the smaller things first. God meets you at multiple places and will never leave you the same when you become open to progressing every day in every area when you welcome Him in, no matter what it may look or feel like.

    I heard God say some things to me that religious people would not agree with, but He met me when others did nothing but judge me outwardly instead of looking inwardly and comforted me by talking to me to eventually win my heart. I am forever grateful that He won my heart and not man. As you progress in your relationship with Him, He will continue to speak, but also in different ways, so be open to feeling and hearing Him speak from within. There will come a time of progressing from the filter that you once had in to hold that old coffee to now exchange it for a new filter, accept it. Allow God to replace the whole thing that the world has filled you up with, and ask Him to replace it with the luxurious brand of ground coffee that is good for your heart, spirit, soul, and mind.

Chapter 10:

The Process

I just know some of y'all skipped to this part; if you did, go back and read from where you started because it's a process to get here, big dawg, lol.

Growing Pains.

It was homecoming week, y'all, and I went to an HBCU, so it was going to be lit, but the only thing was that I was now living a life for God. I wondered if it would still be lit being sober or having no sex. I was in the process of letting God detox my learned habits from all things that I once found comfort in while I was in isolation with Him. I didn't text the people I used to mess with back, but the old girls that either graduated or transferred started to call my phone. I was sitting in bed the night before one of the events and received a FaceTime call early in the morning, so I answered without looking to see who called that earlier in the morning, and it was one of them. She then asked if she could come upstairs to have sex, but my spirit spoke the word "no" before I could even let my flesh ponder. I was then awake for a little bit, crying because of how hard it was. Asking God, "Why do I have to give this up completely while dudes just have to wait for a moment? Shoot, they don't even do that, but my sin causes me to give it up completely?! That's some b..." And it was almost like He knocked me to sleep before I got the rest of the words out.

I woke up knowing my new friends who graduated were coming to town that day, and I started to get ready for the event. I received text messages from more girls asking if I would be able to meet them, but I didn't respond. We got to the event and went in, and I saw at least 3 of them, and it hurt because I knew that I could no longer have them because my heart was now with the mender of the heart that was broken by some of them. It hurt, and I felt anger seeing my guy friends being able to talk to girls and not be judged to go to hell, but instead, shined on by God for finding a good thing that I could not have because it was an abomination. We walked outside and talked to people and saw a fight ending, but I continued to talk with people until I saw one girl who looked at me, and it hurt so bad that I could not talk to her.

We then started walking to the car, and tears started to unravel at every step from a place I thought was sealed. I got weaker in my legs and finally released my tears onto the shoulder of my loving teammate. I then found myself feeling surrounded, protected, and vulnerable, even with people in the distance. What I felt was real. I found myself now surrounded by my loving teammate and friends, crying after I surrendered all this pride of my pleasures to God. No one quite understood what I was going through, but they loved me through it by hugging me or laying their hands on me in that moment and praying for me. My teammate wiped my tears and comforted me by saying in her kind and loving voice, "Bri, I don't understand what you are feeling because I haven't experienced this before, but we are here for you and love you so much."

I think it is a beautiful thing when someone admits they don't understand.

> **In the world we live in, the growth of pride is "freeing" people to say things that God would tell us not to say.**

Words are so powerful, and it is important in certain moments to just be honest and know when to give words and not to. If you haven't been through certain things, I believe it is necessary to just admit that you don't know what they are going through, because that is the very thing they may need to hear in order to receive love from you. Faith always has growing pains. God is already taking them through growing pains, so don't be the person to subtract something that God is in the process of multiplying.

I Want Both Though!

1 Peter 5:6-9

Some of you have gotten to this point and asked, "Why can't I have both though?" and I will explain why with a series of questions I need you to answer honestly.

- If you are entering into a relationship, are your first thoughts, "I am about to cheat on this beautiful person for being so good to me and holding me down through thick and thin"? *(Hopefully, you said no.)*

- If you were in a relationship, would you grow and progress in your relationship? *(Hopefully, you would.)*

- If you were in a relationship, would your significant other tell you things they will and will not tolerate over time because they are overall harmful to who you will become? *(Hopefully, they do.)*

When I fully gave my life to God, what I struggled with for so long was the battle of wanting both the things that I used to have and God. I wanted to have God and girls, God and sex, God and drugs, God and alcohol.

> **The question that God asked me was, "Are you becoming a new person to remain a cheater?"**

Of course, I said no, but dang, that slapped me because I wanted both though! Eventually, as I continued to grow and walk in my relationship with Him more by spending more time in silence, He revealed why it was important for me to depart from trying to have both. He told me, "You cannot have life and death; you cannot have poison and the antidote both dwelling in the same temple/body at the same time because it will eventually kill you. If you let me detox you from everything that may cause death, it will be a benefit to your eternal life."

To live for God is to pursue holiness.

It may feel good temporarily to do all these things that are a pleasure to yourself, but in the end, I'd rather detox and accept Life. I used to want death all the time because it felt so good to satisfy me, but it still left me empty inside. I was that person who, if a "Christian" said, "You are going to hell for sinning," I said, "Send me; I'll go!" I was truly in love with death and hated anything to do with life because people rarely showed me their love with The Life, Jesus. I just saw a lot of fake people that masqueraded around claiming love for someone with no actions through that love being revealed through them. What I didn't understand in my immaturity then is that everything is spiritual; behind the curtain of the physical realm, there is a spiritual one, meaning things are either angelic or demonic, further meaning that eternally there is a choice of entering the gate of Heaven or entering the gates of hell. Now, getting a chance to see demons manifest through people is more proof for me to know this to be the true reality. You cannot have both, you have to choose one.

Face Reality

2 Corinthians 4:18

Ephesians 6:12

Colossians 2: 16-17

In the silence, God will speak to you! So many times, instead of overcoming the silence, we let the voices and discomfort of the silence overcome us. This is why there are a lot of suicides that occur in the world.

> **In the silence, people do not overcome this uncomfortable thing that is for their ultimate breakthrough, because they can be overtaken by a vulnerable spot in the breaking.**

I sat by my mom, crying tears that hurt my spirit, when she told me that this dude, who was about my age and that I knew through our families, had committed suicide. When I first found out, I remembered being in Little Rock and running into him a few months prior. I proceeded to say to him, "Watsup, big dawg, how are you feeling?" and he told me that he was cool, and that was that. I told him to have a blessed day and walked off. Though I did not really know him, it really hurt me to hear that someone's words had the ability to cause anyone to do something of that magnitude. After I cried beside my mommy and went back in the room, I asked God why, and He showed me two important things that I will share with you.

There is so much power in the words that you speak, so make sure that they are used to encourage and uplift people around you. Proverbs 18:20–21 says, "From the fruit of their mouth, a person's stomach is filled; with the harvest of their lips, they are satisfied. The tongue has the power of life and death, and those who love it will eat its fruit."

The second thing God told me is that there is either a breaking or a breakthrough that will happen in silence, or both. So many times, people will never sit through the discomfort of silence because it causes them to be alone with their thoughts. To conquer this silence, you must face reality by opening your eyes to see.

So many times, we remain blind to healing because we want to continue the same cycle of feeling things that are familiar to us. Yup, I said it! You want to feel a temporary satisfaction that will not benefit your eternal salvation. You have the ability to see, but you like the feeling of living as a blind child of pride, so you don't face reality. When God opened your eyes to see, instead of coming out from among them, you chose to close your eyes because it was comfortable. The reality is that God created the earth and made us in His image, meaning we are spiritual beings, citizens of Heaven, and there is a very real spiritual realm. Are you so prideful to think that reality is the world that You alone can physically see? Where is your faith? Is your faith found in you? Are you the author and the finisher of faith? The Kingdom of Heaven is the only reality that we need to seek and that requires faith in Jesus. There is a reason why Jesus says in Matthew 6:10, "your Kingdom come, your will be done, on earth as it is in Heaven." Heaven is a spiritual place that is the standard, and to face reality, you must know and come into agreement with the reality of all things. The reality of all is spiritual and not earthly or carnal. There are so many things that come when you are aware of this, because now you will have the understanding coming from the Lord.

Silence forces you to see the reality of the source of all things, which is the spiritual realm. To face the reality of things is spiritual first, and can either be a divine appointment with God or any dark spirit. When people do not want to face reality, from the lens of pride, they see their reality on earth, and as a result, relationships fail because you do not face the reality of things. You want to continue to look past the dark spirit that you are seeing in this person that you are in a relationship with instead of hearing God. You want to continue blaming everyone who has left you instead of removing pride and avoiding the spirit within yourself. This is why you see the other person as the problem; so many times, you have a lens of pride and do not face reality.

Admit it, you are blinded by pride, because if you weren't, it would be hard to be prideful when you face reality. You are continuing to build the Tower of Babel in the spirit by ignoring God in the silence and making war with God. When you are blinded by pride, you will not see yourself in the wrong because you are not allowing God in. Jesus is the door, and you have a choice: let Him into the silence or continue to not face reality. The reason people run from silence is because they fear the voice of God or the voices they may hear in their heads. Instead of embracing fear of the Lord and facing it, people run and find other things to busy themselves and miss the things that God is trying to show them.

When it comes to hearing voices in your head, at one time, I experienced this and started to speak the Word of God from confidence over my life and pray in silence. Any dark spirit must bow at the feet of Jesus Christ, so do not ignore the silence, but embrace it and discern which is the voice of God. Have a fear of the Lord and not a fear of silence, because healing and breakthrough come in the silence. In 1 John 4:18 it says, "There is no fear in love, but perfect love cast out all fear...", and that understanding comes with knowing who Love is, God is Love. Surgeries require silence and stillness, and for God to do these things in your life, you must face reality.

Chapter 11:

Silent Progression

In the Silence

When I told my parents that I was in relationships with girls, I felt so distant from my family because they didn't understand, so I remained quiet. I didn't know whether to be open or not, but something drew me further from including them in that part of my life. The further I drifted away was the louder these voices became. I heard voices tell me, "They won't understand, so just keep being around people who do," so I did. I went deeper into silencing my true desire to speak to my family. I went because this voice was now speaking this into my heart, so I listened for years. Every year, I chose to put a piece of tape on my mouth even though people said I was speaking my truth, but for some reason, I knew that my truth was just a counterfeit. When I spoke up on campus and joined an LGBTQIA+ group, there was still something missing that I could not put a finger on. Eventually, this community that I loved became distant to me. I started growing an interest to join an D9 greek organization because my friends were in them, but something held me from going through with it. I still didn't feel like I belonged anywhere; I felt like a person who didn't fit into anything. I continued in and out of more situationships in hopes of finding more, but I never did. Could these girls leaving and the loneliness I felt mean something? Was I being called by something bigger than me?

I went to church in hopes of an answer, but I was met with more judgmental eyes, not words of direction, but instead just yelling and shouting. I felt like my spirit needed more and wanted to speak, so I fed myself Scripture and was taught and encouraged by God. I then started talking. I went on a few days' tangents, fell back off to go back to what I knew, and then back on my inspirational Bible revelation tangents, every time back was longer.

Yes, I fell back into what I knew in the in-between. Little did I know that God was using that as a way for me to start to speak for that thing that I knew was bigger than me, and it felt so good when I spoke not about me or a community, but instead about the One who created me.

I found that thing, but I knew I didn't want to give up my lifestyle yet. I was too deep in it, but I knew the future would be bright for this. I would look on this Bible app to check for encouragement from the sermons I wrote when I was younger by saying, "I will just use this in the future." I saw a lot of gay pastors, but I knew that was not what I could ever do. I was so convicted by God when I spoke at a church event for teenage girls because I was in sin currently and because I had messed with someone who was there in the past. I was in college when that happened, and I just knew that could not happen again.

When I gave my life to God fully, I was quiet and isolated from everyone on campus for weeks and loving being in God's presence. After that time, I remember being with my loving teammate, and her friend, who is now my sister, came by her dorm room, and I told her my testimony. I think it was funny because we sat there for hours, and she was shocked because she had seen me on campus in the past, hairline and all. When I said that to them, it was a key that opened the first of doors through not remaining silent. I finally overcame it.

In the future, God told me, not even 4 months after giving my life to Him, to start a event for young adults on campus every week. This then turned into a small ministry on campus with five of my friends that lasted for at least 4 hours most nights. Another pair of keys were found, and the doors opened. Being obedient to what God wants will open doors, no matter how small they may look. My silence is connected to my releasing into the earth what God requires me to. I know my silence will be all broken, and the residue of tape will be released, as I am obedient in releasing what God requires of me.

Identity Theft

John 10:7-11

The devil is the person who steals people's identities because He knows that if it is found in God and submitted to God's will for your life, it means you gain something that he no longer has access to. The devil wants you to continue to feast in front of the tree that Eve ate from (reference to IDOLATREE in Chapter 1) because if you do, pride blinds you and keeps you in the same cycle of falling and being destructive.

When identity in God is no longer present in His creation, there will always be room for perversion and confusion of who and what His creation's true identity is.

Pride consumes God's creation by that creation making themselves the creator and rulers of their own compromised identity that is rooted in pride.

Perversion has corrupted the identity and minds of a lot of people through organizations and systems that was not founded on the only firm foundation, Jesus.

For identity theft not to occur in your spirit and soul, there needs to be knowledge and submission to wanting the Truth instead of the liar, satan. So many times, we want to keep our identity, which is, in a broad sense, being a child of pride. The world loves this mask that has been put on and has blinded us to the Truth. We love to decorate those masks with labels that are what we name ourselves out of a blurred lens and no longer identify with the words God calls us. We choose to submit under the identity or title we name ourselves out of our pleasure and pride instead of aligning our identity and titles with being submitted and further aligning with God and the Promise you deserve. How may you ask? You submit under the label of a "Christian" as an adult and become so pride-filled that you no longer identify with being called a Citizen of Heaven and a Child of God. You submit under the label of being gay or any letter on the growing spectrum, and become blinded by pride to no longer identify with being whoever God calls you, created you, and needs you to be. You submit under the label of being an "ex-addict" and become so pride-filled to think that it was your work that has kept you sober instead of knowing that to remain sober requires 1 Peter 5:6–11.

I am not saying that identifying where you are is bad, but I am saying that people are getting stuck in the label instead of walking into whatever God says about them, and faith is required for that. God told Abram that He was going to be the father of many nations even when he didn't have a son, but because of his action of aligning himself with what God said, he was able to receive that promise. So, when God calls us by name, some action was initiated for us to identify with that title. **Labels created by the world are limiting and sustained by the pride you take in that thing.** Labels that are in alignment with who God calls you will help you identify where you are or show a part of who God called you to be. Identifying yourself as certain things that were experienced can allow for pride to grow and will further limit you from being everything that God called you to be.

When I was labeled in the world as a gay/lesbian golfer, that was a thing that became a limit. Though I enjoyed doing a lot of other things that people can attach labels to, I tried to fit into a box that I was never supposed to be close to. We sometimes attach and identify as the experiences we need on our unique resume for our overall destiny. My identity then was in my sexuality, but that experience was not supposed to become my destiny; instead, it was something I needed to go through. My identity then was that of a golfer, but that experience over the last nine years was not my destiny; instead, it was something I needed for my destiny. "All things work together for the good of those who love God and are called according to His purpose" (Romans 8:28). Why do we attach a label when God is just trying to add it to our résumé?

Prideful pleasures can stop us in the middle of the experience and label it as our overall identity and destiny. It is easy to allow others to label who you are, but it takes boldness and surrender of pride to stand firm in who God already equipped you to be.

My soul and identity are too expensive to give them up for half price.

When you knowingly or unknowingly sell your soul to the devil, you are cheaply giving yourself away because you weren't aware that you were bought at a high price. You were already paid for with the blood of Jesus. I was born as a slave to sin because I was born into a sin-filled world. I would want someone to see me and my potential and pay a lot for me to be free. Why would you continue to stay in bondage when you have the ability to be delivered from that?

The devil has tried to steal your identity by getting you to identify with vices that are not in alignment with receiving God's promise for your life. Identity should never have a destination of dysfunction attached to it. When I stopped finding my identity in the temporary things and agreed to attach it to the only perfect one, God, everything changed. I no longer find my identity in my sexuality, nor do I take action to allow that to be an identifier or label in my life, but I find my identity in God. This is not my opinion, but instead, something I know that if you do this, it will shift the trajectory of your life as it has mine. I don't find my identity in being an alcoholic, smoker, homosexual, golfer, athlete, or addict because I join with the pure things that God wants me to be and allow myself to have my identity fully found in God. As I continue to walk in closer relationship with Him, He continues to bring healing and deliverance to my true identity, that was suppressed by the world, while revealing the reasons that I truly identified with these labels. I am whoever He says that I am because He knows me better than I think I know myself.

Chapter 12:
Building Below The Surface

Build below the Surface

I was sitting in my car talking to this powerful woman of God, and there was confusion that God brought to my remembrance of something spoken over me a few days prior, so I felt the urge to ask. What she told me next really gave me a new perspective on what God does before things start becoming visible to others.

She said in a simple way to me, "Do you think a big building needs to be sturdy?" "Of course!" I said.

The only way that a tall building can be built to sustain all the floors above is to have floors established below the surface.

You cannot expect God to just give you all these deep things if you are not willing to go deeper into your relationship with Him. The places that God needs to take you require experience, and that requires lower levels, so when He does exalt you and build you up above the surface, you will be ready. So do you want to wait on God to continue the work that no one has seen before, or would you rather not be sustained in it?"

I just sat there with no words; I was put on mute. Then I said, "Welp, here we go, God." The process began deeper than I thought.

So many times, we can be so fed up with complaining about where we are and forget the perspective of, "God, what are you currently showing me?" He calls on His children to have a deeper standard. Most people who "blew up overnight" to the world had a process, whether life events or work ethics, established in a low place to get to that exalted place by God today. The rest of these people were high one day, and the next, no one knew about them because of their lack of preparation. You have to allow the building to happen below the surface and before the promise is revealed externally for others to see.

Through the Progression

Acts 8 & 9

My bro Saul was out there murdering people back in the day, for real! He believed only in the Torah (the first 5 books of the Bible), and everyone else in his mind was preaching another doctrine. I would encourage you to read it because it was wild! He was on the road to Damascus, going to arrest and probably murder some more believers of Jesus, and suddenly he encountered Jesus. Jesus blinded him for 3 days, and he had to wait for Ananias to heal his eyes.

I found it interesting that this prophetic sign and miracle were performed because, in the first part of the book, I explained how, in Genesis 3, it was the closing of spiritual eyes and the opening of eyes to see the world's temptation. Paul's spiritual eyes were now open, and his eyes rooted in pride were closed. Notice that Paul did not just receive sight as soon as his encounter with Jesus; he lost it, and there was a process that came through prayer and fasting that led to him receiving His new sight.

God had to shut his eyes to pride that was killing people who believed a different thing or had a "different denomination" than him, and God opened his eyes to know Jesus. This shows us that we are one body of Christ, and division in everything, not aligning with righteousness, is rooted in pride because if it does not align with what you or your denomination sees, then it is not right, so it is not there. It murders through the most powerful thing we have: our mouths. Reading the Bible, I see that there are a lot of things that happened then that are still happening today.

Wanting to progress is the first step. So many people get to a certain age and say they are "too old," when instead, God has you here for a purpose, and maybe it is to allow Him to break down those generational cycles and curses so they will not be passed down to your children's children. Do not continue to sit in comfort, knowing that you are able to give and receive more love, joy, and patience from those around you.

God can only heal the things that you reveal to Him!

Listen to God and ask Him, "What are you trying to do through me right now, God?"

Shift Some & Progress Everyday

There was a religious crowd that wanted to stone that woman, and I always wondered, "Where was the man, though?" "Why do people point at certain people to get other eyes off them?" "Why do religious people now point the finger at the LGBTQIA+ community?"

"Why do we become so comfortable using our mouths to place word curses on others because they do not believe the same thing as us?" "Why do we judge others' sins when they are different from our own?" "Why do we feel that we are able to tell someone they are going to hell?" PRIDE is the answer to all the above.

We are shifting out of that today and shifting our hearts and minds to align with the promises for us found in God. Yes, and Amen. You are stepping into agreement with the words that God speaks over your life, not the words and actions that people place on you. You are not what they called you, but instead, you are a Child of God who is beautifully and wonderfully made in His image. I am sorry that you had to experience the pride that is still in people, and I want you to know that person or group is not how everyone else is. God loves you so much and wants you to grow into a deeper relationship with Him. He loved me through all my tears and the nights I cried myself to sleep, and He will do the same for you. If He did work in me, I know that He can do so much more through you following Him.

Jesus showed them the pride they picked up before the stone was even touched, and I know that if you give Him a chance, He would love to be your Defender. In John 8:10–11, Jesus asked the woman where they went.

Calling out pride drives out everything and replaces it with His promise.

She said to Jesus that no man was there to condemn her anymore. Jesus then tells her, "Neither will I condemn you, so go and sin no more." What does it look like to "sin no more?" It looks like giving up and giving everything you thought was yours completely back to Him. "The earth is the LORD's, and everything in it, the world, and all who live in it" (Psalms 24:1), and that includes you. If you continue to fight Him, He will give you a choice, just like He gave me—life or death.

Now, He changed the identity that I found in sexuality to the identity found in Him. I don't need the labels of the world now that I am a child of God. Let me make it very clear: I am no longer a slave to sin, but I am a child of the Most High God. I am still progressing daily. I do not have sex with people outside of marriage anymore. I do not drink, smoke, or pop pills anymore because I have found that God is better than any counterfeit could ever be. The first shift was me saying yes to whatever God wanted to do with my life, and it was that shift that turned into progressing every day.

On this journey, there has been a lot of things that has come to tempt me again, but I choose the Tree of Life daily. I would encourage you to pray this:

Prayer
"God, I repent, and I need you! Come into my life and shift me into

alignment with the promises that You have for me."

Age is Nothing But a Number.

I went on another "Christian trial run," thinking that dressing differently and wearing different hairstyles would change everything. This time, God planted a seed that started to grow deeper in the ground.

I went to my last college internship in Cleveland, OH. My aunt and I drove to this new job and I saw my male best friend from high school. We spent a few weeks together before he had to go to the new school, so for his birthday, I just told him to pull up at my new job. They came, and I met a few girls there, but one of them stuck out for some reason. After me and him hung out again, I asked him about her, and he gave me a look and said, "No, Bri, she is different. She believes in God."

I didn't know why at the time, but I was supposed to reach out to her. So many times, I always thought the feeling of talking to a girl was perverted for my own gain, but this time, for some reason, my intentions were pure. I was not blind to seeing beauty, but I didn't see her in that way; instead, for the first time, I saw a sister.

Yes, she was younger than me, and God used her in a powerful way in my life as I released that pride and listened to the wisdom within her.

So many times, the thing holding your ego back from listening to someone is someone's age.

In 1 Timothy 4:11–12, Paul tells Timothy not to let anyone look down on him because of his age, but he needs to set an example in his actions that further sets him apart. I am not saying to listen to everyone, but I am saying that age does not matter when someone has been in a secret place with God. That person's actions and speech will show you the wisdom that God has placed on the inside of them to help you heal. So many people will miss the blessing or correction that is necessary for growth because pride and ego stand in the middle. You don't want to listen to someone younger than you because you hold your wisdom in the palm of your hands. Your problem is that you don't want to accept that age is nothing but a number. You can be an old fool. If you have not yet overcome and you speak from a posture of fear from these years instead of perseverance, it is not wisdom. The thing that you have called wisdom is just prideful knowledge because the "beginning of wisdom starts when you have a fear of the Lord" and not a fear of the world (Proverbs 9:10).

Seeing past age causes someone to humble themselves and listen to someone younger than them because they overcame the very cycle you have been in for years. "Humble yourself and sit down" (Jeremiah 13:17-18). Listen to what God is trying to share with you through people. Age is nothing but a number.

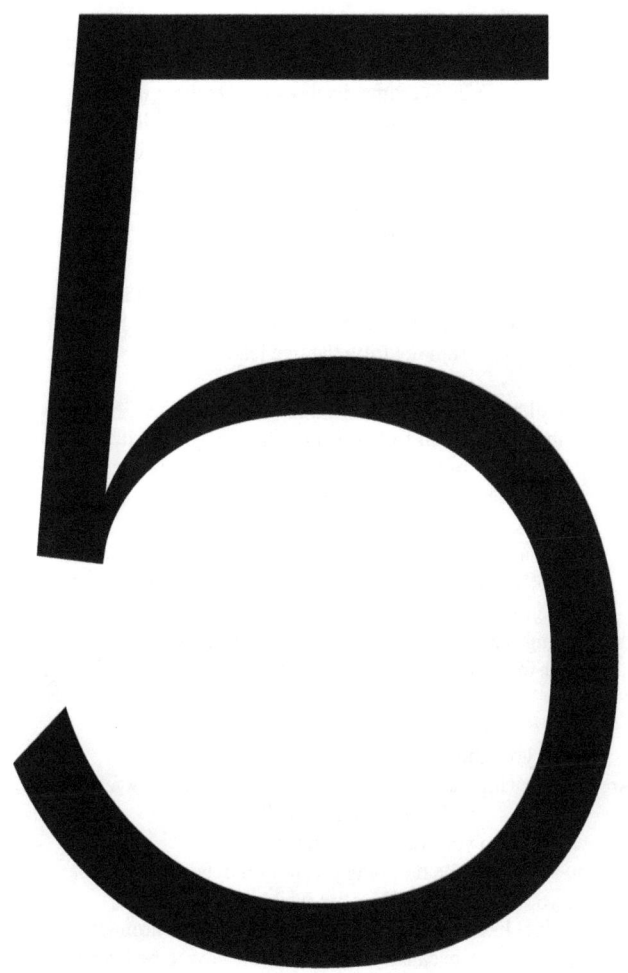

Part Five
PROMISE

STEP INTO THE PROMISE

Internal visibility before external manifestation

External Glimpses overtime display the potential promise
But We pollute the promise process with...Pride
Our eyes rise to see the "I" in the middle of the night
We call our darkness...light
We become a thief in the night
We miss the bright and Morning Star

Taught to Reject and demolish all things that seem far
Far from our opinion that are not in accordance to our religion...I mean tradition
Far from the truth that we learned
Failing to open our eyes
Failing to admit that our fathers inherited lies
Lies that has kept all from opening their eyes to realize
The prince of the air that we have been heirs to
The heir on this earth is darkness

The air that we breathe has been compromised
The things consumed continue to blind our eyes
The things we think... take us deeper into sleep
Thinking we have knowledge and are woke from sleep
Further forgetting that sleep is a form of consciousness

Are you awake from slumber?
Are your thoughts always in a state of wonder?
Are you growing numb from the feelings that you now feel?
Do you want to heal?
Do you want a redirected wheel?
Do you search for the numbing cream or maybe even a pill?
Do you feel consumed by life weighing you down?
Do you feel like there is no hope when people are around?
Do you love others because you never knew how to be loved?
Do you serve below because you have been so traumatized to look above?

All this healing comes from The One whose definition is Love. God.
All challenges are overcome when you decide to take a Step into The Promise

~BRIAHNA WILLIS~

Chapter 13:

Step Into the Promise

"How you gone scare me, I don't even walk by sight... That's what they can't see!"
-Childlike CiCi-

I am currently writing this part in January of 2024, and I need you to know that God has been so good to me. All He requires of us are "Yes" & "Amen," spoken and acted out in faith. I am always trusting in God because He is my Provider and Sustainer. In August, God led me to quit my job, which will be discussed further in my golf testimony book, but God was telling me that I was taking time to do everything but to finish writing the book. During the first few months, I rested, healed, and spent more time with Him, and He provided through people every month for rent to be paid. I tried to go ahead of God's order by starting my golf business first, and that has not worked because He told me to finish writing. I even was going to get another job, but God said no. I wondered why God would not let me, and He continued to tell me that other successes are attached to the simple acts of obedience that He calls us to. To the worldly eye, not having a job is seen as weird and lazy, similar to people who are biblically sound. Now I have graduated by always getting bashed with Leviticus 20:13, and then I am now getting bashed with every verse that you can think about with the word "work" in it (laughs). What I will say is, if God told you to do it, then be obedient to God and not man because "This foolish plan of God is wiser than the wisest human plans, and God's weakness is stronger than the greatest of human strength" (1 Corinthians 1:25, NLT). This is why you must continue to make sure you have luxurious ground coffee (refer back to Replace the Whole Thing! in Chapter 9) and good deposits into your bank, spirit, every day!

He kept paying my rent until my safety was breached, so He told me He wouldn't pay it anymore, and He would take care of me if I just trusted Him in this process. God told me to keep a small portion of things and to give everything else away, so I did. Shortly after, I received an eviction notice and a court date, so I went. He told me to focus on finishing the book even though this and more were happening, so I did. I then received a call saying they needed to do a lockout on the apartment, but I reasoned, and they gave me two more days. That is God's grace. I have never been at this point before myself, but I know that God "will make a way in the wilderness and rivers in the desert" (Isaiah 43:19) when you are obedient to what He tells you to do. I am currently finishing the instruction that He gave me while sleeping in my car, persevering through the adversity. I also know that He created time and can change any circumstance in a millisecond, and my Father has the streets paved with gold in Heaven, so I know He has everything I need, including the non-tangible things. So many times, we can think about the things that we want to gain as inheritance, but we do not realize that for something to be sustained for a long time, God has to remove and strip certain things we were once privileged to have. When He stripped me of certain things and humbled me to a different degree, I am able to now see how every day is so important because you have new mercies every single morning. I sit here calmly thinking about how good God is, realizing that the lower He takes me, the more I experience the fruit of Him to a different degree in this humbling time.

Overall, I trust that God will be my Healer, Sustainer, Provider, and Protector on a different level this season. To some, that may sound stupid, but that is because it derives from the comfort of having the lens of the world on and not yearning and being desperate to see through the lens of the Creator. All I am doing is just allowing Him a chance to do something new, because if I could try a new strain of weed back then, why wouldn't I try something new when He tells me to try with Him? I know God to be my Healer, Deliverer, Sustainer, Protector, and Provider, and since I truly have faith, why would I doubt Him now?

I would encourage you to ask God what your next step in faith looks like and watch Him turn it around. The promise is not just tangible things, but Him taking you into the promise of receiving the fruit of the Spirit being: "love, joy, peace, patience, kindness, goodness, faithfulness, gentleness, and self-control" (Galatians 5:22–23). I am so grateful that God did not give me what I thought I wanted first, such as influence, money, wealth, businesses, and the ministry. He knows me better than I know myself because He sees the future, and He wants all things to have a foundation in Him that will be sustained and remain in Him as I stay close to Him.

Receive It!

Receiving the promises that you deserve goes far beyond physical things. On this journey and in my relationship with God, I have received so much from remaining in Him by learning how to release control. For so long, I didn't see beauty in myself because I always relied on people to say it. I never looked at myself fully in the mirror and saw the very beauty that My Creator handcrafted while I was in my mother's womb until now. I believe it is just a bonus when others say it because God is changing my default to let His words be the things that matter most. Furthermore, God has protected my peace in the middle of the things that He has seen happen in my life. When He told me to sleep in my car, He was the one who overwhelmed me with peace and joy in the middle of what people see as chaos. I started receiving the promise when I closed my eyes from seeing out of the lens of the world and allowed God to open them by believing in the unseen and having faith.

The process of receiving the promises that you deserve is activated when your sight and understanding end.

If you understood everything, whose understanding would you lean on? If you saw everything, who would open your eyes to the spiritual?

The thing that cannot go on this journey is pride, because everything else stems from it. If you believe that you are able to give yourself the promises that you deserve, then that makes you ruler of yourself. Yes, we were made in His image and likeness, but that does not make you the lord of your own life. If you were the lord of your own life, why are you still searching for the purpose of life? Why are you still having to fill yourself with perverted things that will leave you empty? You have to drop this pride to receive the promises that you deserve.

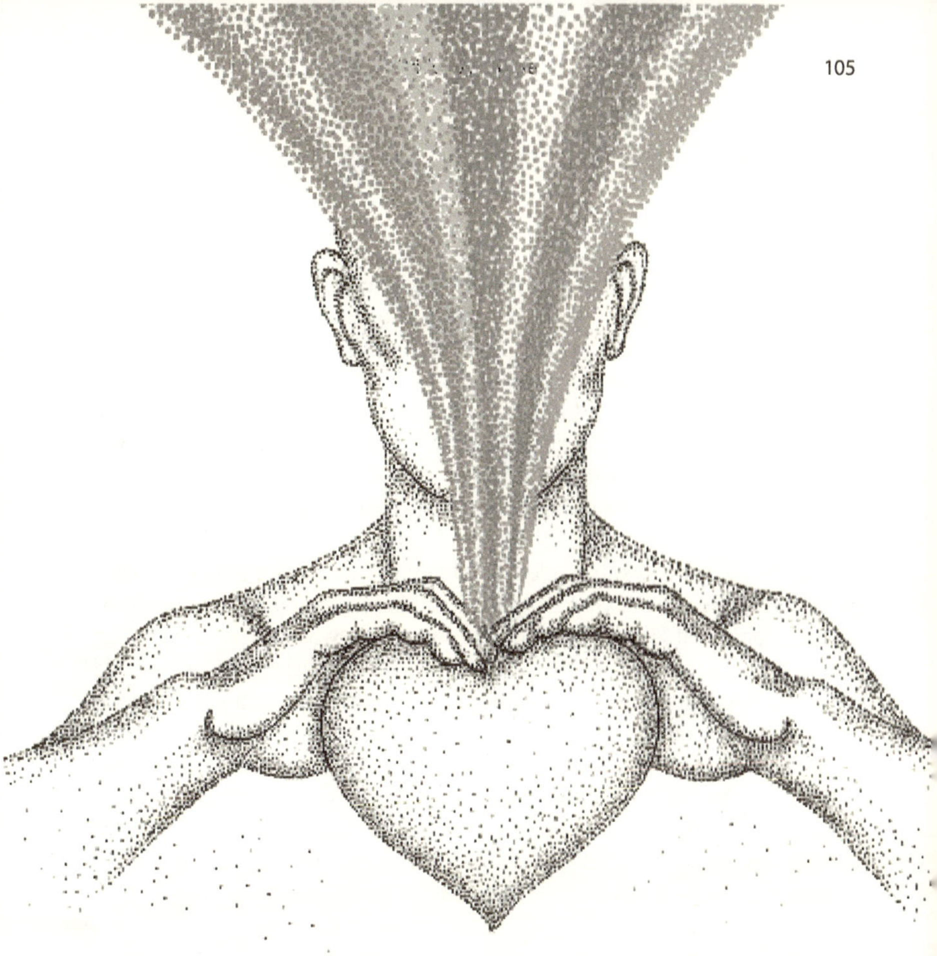

Chapter 14:

Internal Promise First!

The Persevering & Preserved Process to Receive the Promise

Genesis 6-9

God will give you the promise and covenant as you walk in obedience to the things He called you to do. So many things that God asks us to do are simple, but we make them more complicated than they have to be. God told me to write this book, and I made it so much more complicated than it needed to be. God wanted me to give my life to Him years before, but I just said, "One more girl, one more blunt, one more pill, some more lean, one more video." That is what I told God. That one more time led me into another cycle lasting many more years.

My bro Noah was surrounded by a lot of things that are going on today, as it says in Genesis 6. God saw the thoughts and imagination of the heart in the people that He created and now saw that it was only evil, but Noah found grace in the eyes of the LORD. God then instructed Noah to build an ark with certain materials because He was going to send a great flood to wipe everyone and everything else out, so Noah obeyed with that in mind. God said that He would then, after that, establish His covenant, or in other words, His promise to Noah. Afterward, all of this happened. I wonder what obstacles Noah had to overcome in order to fulfill this promise. Were people telling him that he was crazy for listening and building based on something that he had yet to see? Probably.

After Noah finished, they went to preserve the male and female animals of every species and took them inside the ark alongside his family. Noah finished doing all that God commanded him to do, and then the Lord told Noah to go into the ark because, in seven days, He would send rain that would last for 40 days and nights. After the flood and the water were washed away, the ark rested on the mountain. They waited longer for the waters to wash away by sending a raven first, followed by doves, and finally, the dove brought an olive leaf. Later, they got out of the ark, and God told them, "Behold, I establish my covenant with you, and with your seed after you" (Genesis 9:9). God goes on to give a sign to Noah by saying, "I have set my rainbow in the cloud, and it will be the sign of the covenant between me and the earth. Whenever I bring clouds over the earth, and the rainbow appears in the clouds, I will remember my covenant between me and you and all living creatures of every kind" (Genesis 9:15).

The first thing that God showed me in this was that His promise is for all of His children to get a choice to experience, but His promises require a "yes" and an "Amen" fully in our lives. Noah did not conform to the things going on around him but instead chose to live a life fully consecrated to God for God's promises to be established through Him. This was a journey that Noah embarked on to see a promise and instead granted an everlasting one over his life and the generations that followed.

The second thing that God showed me was that in order for Noah to experience the promise, there had to be perseverance present. That man was around 500 years old when God was talking to him about building the ark, and I know people were clowning him and his family while he was building. Similarly, now, some people will not understand why and how God will tell you that but offer their own opinion on certain things in mind and words, remember that your perseverance is necessary for the promise that God has for you.

The third thing that God showed me was that He had to preserve (keep) Noah's family and the animals for a season while God worked out the rest outside the place, which was not safe for him to be in yet. I know so many times I get into a place and try to rush out of it now, but God just needs you to allow Him to do the work while he makes your environment ready for your arrival. It is hard to wait in the middle of uncertainty, but it is necessary for you to have patience and not get out prematurely.

It's impossible to get to the promise if you are not in the boat that God intended you to be in because only the people who followed God survived and received life. For so long, I wanted to just "make it," but you will never be satisfied without being in alignment with God's promise for your life because He offers the necessities internally to be sustained there, too. I had to stop seeking the counterfeit rainbow that allowed me to find my identity in my sexuality because, when I did that, I started the process of allowing God to build in my life. The moment I chose to release pride, in both ways, He started further guiding me and directing me toward getting to the promise because there are certain steps that need to be taken to fully seek His promise for me.

Breakthrough!

Revelation 12:11

This was my second semester of trying groups at church. I was in college and wanted to be around people who were my age because the first group had older women who judged me. This was my last try, so I prayed about which to join, and one title popped out to me, so I signed up!

A few weeks prior, I started hanging out with my loving teammate and friends more who also followed God. Although I was familiar with seeing them with my teammate, I did not know them for myself. When I slowly came out of my isolation with God after encountering Him, I hung around her friends more and more as my other friends disappeared. I invited my other friends to the campus church, but I was met with ridicule and was trying to be the one to get this girl's number for them. This time, my eyes were opened to the fact that this was childish, and because of my awareness, I had to put it away. Eventually, as I stood firm in God, people drifted. I sat in a quiet place with God for weeks, only going to class, tournaments, and sometimes getting food to go in the cafe. It felt as if I saw a ghost; I saw no one during that time.

My teammate sent another church live, and this time, they talked about groups, so I felt I needed to join one, even after my first experience. This was my last try, so I prayed about which to join, and one title popped out to me, so I signed up! I remember the week leading up to our first session. I received a call from the group facilitator, and she was so sweet. She just called to remind me, pray for me, and speak life into me, and I knew this was different; I was all in. She added me to a group chat full of unnamed numbers, and I saw that two numbers were from Maryland. I now receive a call and text from one of those numbers, with a familiar voice on the other line saying my name, and it registered. Out of all the people in the world that were part of groups, the dude on the other line of this phone call was one of my teammate's friends I just started hanging around with from my school. That was wild!

On the first call for the group, I was heading to the airport to go to another tournament in college. I told the facilitator ahead of time, and she was cool with it. I had my headphones in while listening to everyone pick and choose what they wanted to tell these people they knew nothing about, and I sat quietly listening. He was on the call speaking, so there was peace in knowing someone by association already. I finally got through security with the team but felt a rush to put my headphones on quickly, so I put them on. As I started back walking into the airport to the gate, the first thing I heard the facilitator say was, "Does anyone else want to share anything about themselves before we wrap up the call?" I was stopped in my steps, a pounding in my chest, and words were now clouding my mind on what specifically to say.

I stopped by Jamba Juice with my headphones on and paused because this release was hurting me to do. As I paused in my thoughts that were logically saying no, she said, "Okayyy, we are about to pray," and that was now followed by my spirit speaking first, "I actually want to share right quick, if it's not too late." She gave me encouragement to do so, and

I preceded by saying, "Hey y'all, sorry I haven't been active; I just got through the airport, but Watsup, I'm Briahna Willis! I am from Little Rock, Arkansas, Tha 501, but I go to school in Maryland. I am an D1 collegiate athlete, which is why I am going to be at the airport most of the time for our meetings. I used to be an alcoholic, smoke a lot of weed, and I am just getting out of messing with a lot of women. God encountered me in my room, and I am just trying to progress and be around people who are on that path too!"

That was the most awkward silence that I ever experienced. My heart felt released by saying that, and I was worried that they would also judge me. "Sooo, does anyone have any prayer requests?" said the facilitator. Even people saying their prayer requests after I spoke was awkward, and at this point, I was ready to go, but I waited. As soon as "Amen" came out of her mouth, I removed myself. I was frantic and was going to comfort myself by getting some Jamba Juice until I received a phone call from the dude. My hands were shaking at this point, but I somehow was able to answer by saying, "Hello?" He said, "Bri, thank you for being that vulnerable and bold in sharing that. You did a great job, and that helped me to be more vulnerable in the future." With a confused look and tone, I said, "Uhh, Thank you…"

After that initial session, that weight removed from my heart no longer stayed because I overcame it and received a breakthrough! After that group, my friendship grew with my facilitator and also with the dude.

In the growing and getting to know each other process of our friendship, I felt like I could go to this party, so he and a younger teammate came with me. My first party after I was saved, we went, and they had an event called "Club Inferno" (laughs). As we walked in, everywhere I looked, there was a familiar girl that I knew intimately. My younger teammate left, and it was me and him walking around, sober, while seeing others drunk. Being in this place was not fun, but we walked more, and I ran into a group of girls as the dude had distance from me now. "Awwww, you have been gone for a while, Bri! *laughs* You not selling drinks no more and now you over here not messing with our friends no more because you on this Christian b* now. You a b*!"

I stood there after they walked off, and my face told the hurt I felt. I thought I was spreading the good news on social media, but this is what I receive?! I walked over to him with defeat on my face, and shortly after telling him what happened, they shut things down because of a fight.

On our way out, another girl yells out to me as I am about to get in the car. It was obvious that I knew her, but she was too drunk for me to pay any attention to her words. I knew I had to leave because we had history, and I didn't want to fall again. As I was leaving, it started raining, and I saw two girls walking. I felt that I was supposed to give them a ride, so I asked the dude who was riding with me if he and my younger teammate could make room for whoever the girls walking in front of us were. They both looked at me, and he proceeded to ask, "Bri, are you sure?" Not seeing or knowing why they asked, I said yes. I rolled down my window and was shocked to see who these two were. I just got cussed at by their friends, and now I was supposed to give these tipsy girls a ride?! I just messed with one of them, which is what I was saying to God in this short time frame. Cars were behind me, and another drunk girl that I knew was in the background telling me to hurry up. I just let them get in the car because it was raining. I asked where they needed to go, and they told me their familiar destination. The car ride was filled with giggles, and as they got out of the car, they two said something similar to their friends about me now following Jesus in a way that was the perfect combination.

I went back to drop this dude to his car off at my loving teammates apartment and was on the verge of tears until I got upstairs to tell her what happened. I walked up the stairs and got to him, who blocked the door by telling me that she was sleeping. I couldn't hold these emotions in any longer, and I didn't know him enough to cry. Every step down those three flights was a piece of a shell cracking open, and before the last step, I broke down into tears. I was so weak that I started to cry all over this dude that I barely knew. Snot was everywhere, and tears streamed onto his clothes, and he comforted me in the middle of this persecution. Me and him sat in his car while my younger teammate waited on me in my car. He prayed, and I felt the peace that God gave me through his being a great friend, so we talked more, and I went to my apartment and sat with God.

You break through pride by overcoming with your testimony and by being vulnerable.

Admitting that you are weak is the strongest thing you can do because God is now able to be your strength. He will strategically place people in your life for something that you may not see happening right now. There is an internal promise that God wants you to experience first!

Chapter 15:

SHIFT

Give Up!

Matthew 22:14

You have to give up and move out of the way in order to make way for God because He waits for you to accept Him. "Many people are called, but only few are chosen" (Matthew 22:14). Things happen in life that are devastating. So many challenges that we face in life can be something that has the option to draw us closer to God or further from Him, but it is your choice to either choose the Tree of Knowledge of Good and Evil or the Tree of Life next. Because He calls you to His Kingdom, He will take you through things that you are battling on your own to see if you will drop pride and run into the arms of your Father.

Pre-knowing Jesus. I was on this flight back home at night. I sat next to this lady, and even then, I had never met a stranger. Sometimes, those strangers and I were acquainted in other ways sooner; instead of having actual friends who were girls, I had more intimate relationships with them. This lady then sat beside me. We looked at each other and shared a laugh. I got her number and socials on the flight, and we talked to each other the majority of the time. That was the bumpiest plane ride that I had been on; from the time that plane lifted off to 15 minutes before landing, it was wild, and it is only by grace that I am here today. I was scared for a second, and I know I was not tripping because I heard a lot of people on the flight calling out the name "Jesus," but I was good because I had someone to comfort me physically. We talked more, and I was telling her that I probably just needed a drink, not juice, kids, so the lady came mid-conversation to take drink orders, and she bought us drinks. We finally landed, and y'all, I was so drunk and sick after that flight that I just had to sit and eat. I felt miserable. In the moment, it took my focus off the thing that truly mattered, which was after I landed at the destination.

Your life is like that flight that I took, full of bumps and drops. From the beginning of the ride, we were born into sin, and that was our default, but when bumps and drops come, the question is: who will you turn to for the rest of the journey? Will you cry out to Jesus, or will you distract yourself with alcohol, drugs, knowledge, your business, relationships, men/women, sex, or other things? Take your eyes off of the distraction; trust me, I know it can be, and feel good then because the things that are displayed are temporarily pleasing, but it will not be beneficial when you sit in that chair afterward, wishing you had just not done it.

People want to go to Heaven without being earthly good for The Kingdom of Heaven to be revealed through there lives. I'd rather be on the journey with Him than tip-toe around things that He hates. Yes, we sin and fall short, and we repent, which means turning from those things to worship the Creator of Heaven and Earth, God. Why would I be so pride-filled to think that I would go to Heaven after not even crying out to Him at my lowest point and choose to do my own thing and sprinkle Him in sometimes? You cannot have it both ways (Matthew 6:24). You cannot live a life pleasing yourself and trying to maybe fit God in some way. You need to give up; give your life completely to Him. He knows you better than you know yourself, so accept that and give up.

I am so glad that God did not define my destination on just that flight; instead, He gave me another day and the choice to finally say yes to Him completely. To believe in God is to know Him, and the beautiful thing is that even "atheists" on that plane cried out His name, Jesus. Everyone knows His name; even demons do, and they are fearful of that name because we were made to know His name.

"Every knee shall bow, and tongue will acknowledge God" (Romans 14:11).

Don't let pride hold you back from experiencing the promise God has for you.

Faith

Hebrews 11
Hebrews 12:14-15

Faith requires consecration to God. "Consecration" means to dedicate, to sanctify, or to make holy. For me to dedicate my life to someone, I first need to have faith, and why not just have faith in the Creator of everything? I have tried having faith in people, religion, relationships, and things, but they have all failed me. Why not try something different? When you trusted people, you trusted in something that you didn't see in the future when you chose them, so why not try something different?

When you have and walk by faith, your pursuit of faith is now what allows you to take possession of God's promises that He has for you. The promise is delivered by grace to the door of your life, and the promise can only be accessed through having faith. "We were all saved by grace through faith in Christ Jesus" (Ephesians 2:8–9). The promise is available for you and everyone else because of the grace of God, but it requires faith to possess your promise. It's like having $5.5 billion in your bank account and not taking your portion out of the bank and claiming it.

As you choose to now walk into a deeper relationship with God, faith is required to live a consecrated life. No, it is not living a ritualistic life, but instead asking God to examine you and to live a life that He needs you specifically to live. An example of this is that He told me shortly after my dorm room encounter with Him to stop eating certain foods. At first, I didn't listen and proceeded to have seafood dressing and all the chicken until God revealed Himself in a goofy but fearful way to me, to the point of me stopping that next day. The reason I mention this is because He didn't tell my friends to do the same thing; He just required that of me. Faith is in the things you do not see around you as well, so I now count it as joy. So many times, God can trust you in the word He speaks to you because, even with you not seeing anyone else around, are you going to act and trust what He says? Some people will not understand, but it is not for them to understand; it is for you to just have faith and say Yes to God!

God Chose Me.

Do you answer unknown numbers that look familiar—not spam risks, but just unknown numbers? If you don't, lol, that's probably your problem big dawg. God has been calling your phone for years now! The area code and number is familiar to your eye because you were made to recognize it. He created you in your mother's womb, He knew how you were going to be, and He knows the number of hairs that were and will be added back to your head. He knows you. You have been declining the call from God, but instead going to what seems like comfort in that scenario for years by texting and asking, "Who is this?" You would rather text than answer the call from God. I am that person who just doesn't text back after seeing that sometimes because you did not even save the number with what I gave you. You act like you don't know God, but not saving the number on your phone shows your true relationship with Him. God gave you the gift of His number (His Son) that He gave freely for you to be saved, but it starts when you accept the call and then remove pride and embarrassment by asking, "Who is this?". When He tells you, you have to apologize and tell Him sorry for ignoring Him for so long, and then immediately changes are made in the contacts to being forgiven when you save His number in the phone of your life and hide every text message, His Word, in your heart. As you upgrade, so will the features and how you experience calls from Him because now you can FaceTime. "Many are called, but few are chosen." ANSWER THE PHONE FOR HIM!

There's a movie I watched a while ago; they had winners, and the way they got in contact with them was by calling or coming to their door to inform them of their being chosen. Are you going to open the door of your heart and answer the voice that your soul desires? So many times, we can miss out on the blessing that God has for us because of the past hurt that we have experienced with a number of different people. You may have been hurt in church, and I am sorry for that. Relationships with God are so much different than knowing rituals and religion, so although you were hurt, please pick up the phone again. He is giving you the choice.

I can sit here and act like you have a choice, but it is really about how low you are willing to go before you give up. I tried to run from the call so many times, especially when people would tell me how much of a light I was. The moment that I stepped into the marvelous light is when I wish that He wouldn't have dragged me even by my locs through this, but I am grateful to know that through all of these things that He took me through, I have to know that God Chose Me.

Chapter 16:

Come Out!!!

Everybody Come Out!

2 Corinthians 6:17-18 (KJV)

People are easily caught up telling others what their destination will be instead of lovingly showing them to seek the Kingdom through their own lives as examples. **As followers and disciples of the Most High, people need to do a better job of being a part of people's journey and loving people through their process of growing in relationship with God.** When you make comments such as, "You just need to wear a dress" or "You just need to have sex with a boy; it will make everything better,"

I promise you that is not the solution; you must instead allow God to show others the root. Everything is a process, and when you experience something for so long, you grow comfortable in that way. Some people just go to church every Sunday (some go everyday) to be "good Christians," in the same way that people live an LGBTQIA+ lifestyle. Both are contingent on what "you know" or have grown to want because of the trauma that you have experienced, but so many times, we are not willing to give up our knowing and admit that we know nothing without the Creator.

If you have gotten this far in the book and need a list of things you need to overcome the challenges of life to receive the promises that you deserve, I will list some of the things we talked about in this journey below:

- DROP THE PRIDE AND EGO by admitting that you don't know everything!
- HAVE FAITH in the One who created you.
- FORGIVE YOURSELF
- FORGIVE OTHERS
- KEEP IT REAL WITH GOD about how you truly feel!
- KNOW THERE IS A PROCESS
- TRUST IN THE PROCESS
- The PROMISE is produced in the PROCESS that you persevere through.
- BE OBEDIENT when God tells you to do anything.
- SHARE YOUR STORY... TELL YOUR TESTIMONY to overcome
- DROP THE PRIDE AND EGO by admitting that you don't know everything!
- Yes, I put this one twice ;)

My favorite read to this day, aside from the Bible, is a book called *"Weight Loss the Jabez Way" by Dr. Scott Conrad*. It talks about weight loss, and I used it with that in mind, but he mentions something that was so profound that I will say it the way I received it. If we were to look at the United States, the whole world, the universe, the stars, and the galaxies around us, we would know about less than 1% of everything. Shoot, AI is smart, but it cannot and will not be able to know the number of hairs in your head and tell you about yourself because it doesn't know you. Only God can do that because He created you. On the big percentile of things, we only know 1%. I see a vision of people clinching their fists with "their knowledge and wisdom," even though the things that come from their mouth sound like intellectual fools. Y'all, I admit that I know nothing apart from God and am nothing without having a relationship with God.

Sometimes we clench our fists with the 1% of us knowing the way that we think is right because we pride ourselves in thinking we know all instead of admitting that we are stubborn, pride-filled fools who refuse to listen to someone else. And that's on Proverbs, lol. Might I say that there is only one source of truth to test your theory? There is such a thing as an opinion, but "your truth" is pride that is willing to give up God's will in exchange for your own. He is a gentleman and will respect your prideful decision. The reason there is so much Scripture in this book is because I choose to be wrapped in the Truth, not in my opinion, which is a mask of pride-filled motives for my flesh to remain fed. I choose to have no opinion because I only desire for The Truth to be spoken through me.

Release your 1% into God's hands, and He will give you access to wisdom and understanding of the other 99% that you blocked yourself from receiving. Whatever you think you know, you need to be open to hearing something else, because if you are not open, you can grow certain that "your knowledge" is the only right thing, which in the process, makes "your knowing" the god that you now start to serve. Yes, you have an opinion and something that you may want to do, but submit it to the One who knows you better than you know yourself, big dawg. Be open and do not keep hosting stubbornness because that is the thing holding you back from your promise. What would have happened if Noah had said to God, "Well, according to my calculations, it hasn't rained in approximately 387 days and 5 hours, so with the knowledge that I have, I will not build the ark because that does not align with my truth?" God would not have been able to use Noah to build the ark because, obviously, in that example, he would have known everything. Are we able to admit that we literally know nothing? Yes, Noah probably saw that it hadn't rained, and he was also able to submit the things that he saw because the Creator of everything told him to. The problem is, now that we live in a world that believes they are their own god of knowing, everyone has "their truth". When you find truth in yourself instead of resting in the Truth that He is, it puts you at a crossroads. You cannot serve two masters, God and yourself, so just give up and admit that you are not where you want to be, and the only Way, The Truth, and Eternal Life are found in Jesus Christ.

This is a journey that is not looking for a destination but rather focusing on progress and enjoying the process. People get so caught up in pressing toward a destination that, in the process, they become blind to the purpose of the now, and this is why people are starting to ask about the purpose of life. Pressing is a necessity for the oil to pour out of your life daily. So many people want the destination but do not value the process and the work of getting into the next place that God has for you. Treasure the process, knowing that He will never leave you or forsake you. Yes, you had to go through things growing up, and I understand, but I promise you there is glory on the other side. Keep trusting and having faith in God, because He has to test you in order to trust you with all the seen and unseen blessings that are in store for you. Cry and lean into seeking His face because I know and promise that everything works together for the good; it has to, for His will through your life to be established.

In every area of my life, God has started the process of restoring. For the years that I prayed to have a better relationship with my mom, that is now coming to fruition through communication that may seem uncomfortable. I have also started to have more female friends that I do not see in a perverted way because God is renewing my lens from a worldly perspective to see out of His lens. Looking through the lens of pride will have you blinded by your pleasure and seeing everything and everybody in a perverted way, and you will block the blessing in the process. Some church girls had tried, and many had fallen into sin because of my being a child of pride and not a child of God at the time. Pride comes before the fall, so we are going to spit it out fully and remove it altogether; swallowing pride is not an option if you want to receive the promise.

I also do not need or care to smoke anymore because He filled me with another spirit. The HOLY SPIRIT is my bestie, fasho! When you allow Holy Spirit into every area of your life, it will be a process, but just know that it leads to God's promise for your life.

I know it was not fair what they did to you, and God is calling you to heal with Him instead of going to smoke, use drugs, pop pills, drink alcohol, or have sex—because that is a distraction. He wants you to bring everything to Him so He can heal you if you choose the Tree of Life instead. Let God give you fruit that is sustained, not the ones from the other tree that are counterfeit and will only last for a short time. Instead, eat the everlasting fruit from the Tree of Life. Choose life, not death. Come out of the closet of darkness and into the marvelous light! He is waiting for you to say yes to Him fully. Give your life to Him fully, and if you feel like no one else sees you, KNOW THAT GOD DOES. He wants you to live a life for Him on earth and get the privilege to worship Him in Heaven.

Even though I am currently writing this while homeless and sleeping in my car, I will tell you that He is so worth it because the inner work that He has done in me thus far is beautiful. Yes, there are going to be challenges along the way, but that is a part of the process that I will count as joy, and you get to see soon what the Lord has promised you to bring to fruition. So many times, people can see a promise as the work that is physically seen, but He wants you to experience FREEDOM in your spirit before He gives you the physical things. He took me through all of these obstacles and tested that. At every turn, I wondered if it was worth it, and now I can say that with a life fully surrendered to Him, it is worth it. Knowing and having a relationship with God is worth every tear cried; it has been worth it because, to most, they see chaos in places that God has graced me to have joy during. God has graced me to have peace when others around me worry and try to save me from a place where God wants to show Himself as my Protector. To the physical eyes of the world, it is not wise, but spiritually, with faith, I am confident that exaltation comes from being humbled by God when you are obedient.

The reason I am able to overcome and receive the promise is first through believing, having faith in God, and sharing my story, that God graced me to go through, with you. It was not an overnight thing, but in order for you to overcome anything and receive a true promise, you have to share the testimony that is attached, like Revelation 12:11 says. If you want a different result, I will challenge you to have faith and come out of whatever closet you have stepped into.

So, if you want to give your life to Him completely, pray this prayer:

Prayer

"God, WAKE ME UP! I repent and turn away from the things that I used to do. I admit that I am a sinner, fasho! I need You to change my life completely! I turn away from my old way of living! I need You to guide me on this journey in my relationship with You. I believe and thank You for sending Your only Son, Jesus Christ, to die on the cross for my sins. I repent, God! I come out of the closet of darkness and walk into Your marvelous light! I say yes to Your will and way in my life. I love You! Thank You for saving me from being a child of pride. I give You my life completely to use for the Kingdom of Heaven! I will follow You, praise You, and worship You forever! I receive the promise that You have for me. In Jesus' name, AMEN."

If you gave your life to Christ, I am so lit for you! I would encourage you to start praying and reading the Bible and to stay up-to-date with my social media or other resources that I have available.

Into the Promised Land!

Deuteronomy 12:1-14

For God's promises to come to fruition, there has to be a process that is sometimes difficult but possible to overcome. In order for Him to dwell in places of us, such as our hearts, spirits, and souls, He needs to change and sometimes break certain things that were established by the culture that was once built before God's arrival of wanting to dwell there. We see this in Deuteronomy 12:1–14: God needed that place to be destroyed of anything that had any residue of the old gods and idols that were in that sacred place. This is the same thing that He does in our hearts, spirits, and souls. He needs to do renovations on our temple by surrendering our will fully to Him. They did not keep anything old before God dwelled there fully, but instead destroyed and cut it out. No longer can we live our lives trying to keep certain things that we want because it can hold us back from experiencing the promises that we deserve. No longer will we live a life that tries to hold on to both, but instead, we will give our lives completely to God, surrendering to His perfect will being done.

So many times, He saves us because He doesn't give us what we want since it is not in alignment with His will for our lives. I used to be so pissed at God because I would be broke in college, and I would pray for Him to give me money if He was really real, and He didn't. What I didn't know then, but now know is that it was all working in accordance with His perfect timing because that thing I wanted was not good for me for the next season. Yes, He will allow you the ability to go to certain things, but it's just a matter of knowing that He wants to take you through them.

Our lives consist of the things that take you into a dark tunnel: loss, failed relationships, depression, identity crisis, diagnosis, and addictions that take you deeper into the dark. So many times, we stay in stagnant darkness and call it our dwelling place because that is all we know, so we stay comfortable. If you keep moving and keep progressing, there is an end and a light at the end! It doesn't matter how long you have been crying in the middle of that tunnel; I promise it gets better when you get up and don't rely on your own strength, but this time, walk with God. When you go through, it means you are going into and out of something, but so many times the "coming out" is in our own strength and doing our will instead of His. It looks like you came out, but really, you were at a dim light in the tunnel, and you sat there in that counterfeit light. God wants you to keep walking into the promise and not staying into pride.

Pride will lead you to believe that we alone can serve ourselves as the standard of where we are. Walking into the Promised Land will require you to know that because sin blinds you and leaves you comfortable, the only true standard is found in the Word of God. What you thought was "your truth" about yourself is really just, in actuality, "Your opinion," because there is only One Truth, Way, and road to eternal Life. The reason I say this is because an unsurrendered mind will leave you in that tunnel, sitting there looking at the light that you think is the true one forever. I want to encourage you by saying that you have the ability to walk beside the light in the middle of everything and receive the true gifts that come with knowing Him as your friend!

John 8:12 (NIV)
"When Jesus spoke again to the people, he said, "I am the light of the world. Whoever follows me will never walk in darkness, but will have the light of life."

This true light will guide you into the Promised Land, and I know this for myself.

In Revelation 22:12–16, Jesus is speaking to us. He shows and tells us who He is and also shows us the importance of keeping his commands. When we "wash our robes," or, in other words, are born again, we have rights to the Tree of Life. As we talked about in the first few chapters about the two trees in the middle of the Garden of Eden, they had a choice. Jesus is coming soon, and you have a choice. You can either continue to choose to eat from the tree that was rooted in pride, or you can choose "The Root" (Revelation 22:16), which is Jesus, who is the only way to enter the gates of Heaven. Will you allow pride to continue to blind you from the whole truth because of your partial blindness? Will you admit that you honestly know nothing in comparison to the One who Created you? Will you give up the things that are comfortable and pleasurable to pursue blessings? Will you finally just give up and come to the end of yourself to receive Jesus? Will you allow yourself the opportunity to receive the promises that you deserve? Will you STEP INTO THE PROMISE?

I love you so much. Share this book with someone so that healing can take place in their lives too.

Receive a Free Digital Gift!

Get access to devotionals, discipleship lessons and more!

www.briahnawillis.com/pridetopromisedigitalgift

THERE IS A **PROCESS** TO GET TO THE

PROMISE
PROMISE
PROMISE
PROMISE
PROMISE
PROMISE
PROMISE
PROMISE

...HERE IS THE PROCESS

$25.99
ISBN 979-8-9898428-0-3